The Birdkeep[...]

Senegal Pa[...]

Tammy Gagne

Senegal Parrots

Project Team
Editor: Tom Mazorlig
Copy Editor: Stephanie Fornino
Indexer: Ann W. Truesdale
Series Design: Mary Ann Kahn
Design Layout: Angela Stanford

T.F.H. Publications
President/CEO: Glen S. Axelrod
Executive Vice President: Mark E. Johnson
Publisher: Christopher T. Reggio
Production Manager: Kathy Bontz

T.F.H. Publications, Inc.
One TFH Plaza
Third and Union Avenues
Neptune City, NJ 07753

Printed and bound in China
09 10 11 12 13 1 3 5 7 9 8 6 4 2

Library of Congress Cataloging-in-Publication Data

Gagne, Tammy.
  Senegal parrots / Tammy Gagne.
     p. cm.
  Includes index.
  ISBN 978-0-7938-1479-4 (alk. paper)
  1. Senegal parrot. 2. Poicephalus. I. Title.
  SF473.P3G34 2009
  636.6'865--dc22
                              2009017514

The Leader in Responsible Animal Care for Over 50 Years!®
www.tfh.com

Contents

1

Introducing the Senegal and Its Kin

Parrots are among the most mesmerizing creatures on the face of the earth. They are highly intelligent, extremely social, and possess skills that never cease to impress their many admirers. Parrots fly, they talk, and they capture the hearts of their owners with an intensity once only thought possible by more mainstream pets like cats and dogs. The Senegal parrot and its eight sister species are some of the most gregarious companion birds available for pet ownership. Known for being easy to keep, they offer large parrot perks in small parrot bodies.

The Poicephalus Family

Senegals are members of the *Poicephalus* family. (Scientifically, this is really a genus within the parrot family.) The Greek word *Poicephalus* literally means *made of head.* This is fitting because all poicephalus parrots have large heads, short tails, and stocky bodies. When these little birds were first imported into the United States from Africa, most wild-caught specimens were skittish, panicky, and would often deliver painful bites. Their immediate offspring, however, were entirely different birds. Hand-raised Senegals and other poicephalus parrots are calm, playful, and remarkably tame. Although the size and command of their vocabularies are usually surpassed by those of larger birds (such as African grey parrots), the words that poicephalus parrots learn they learn well.

The Senegal parrot is the most commonly available of the poicephalus parrots.

The visual differences between male and female Senegals are subtle; only veterinary tests can accurately determine the sex of one.

Senegal Parrot

The Senegal is by far the most popular poicephalus parrot in captivity. Known for their pleasant temperaments, Senegal parrots are also adored by pet owners for their pleasing appearance. Most measure only about 9 inches (22.8 cm) long and weigh between 125 and 170 grams, but these conservative dimensions do little to detract from their striking appearance. Primarily green, the wild Senegal is readily able to camouflage himself amid the moist woodlands of his natural surroundings on the edge of the African savannah, but within the home, a captive-bred bird's colors are anything but inconspicuous.

Paired with a bright yellow abdomen and a regal-looking gray hood, the green that covers the remaining parts of the body is electrified as part of the feathered Senegal suit. The green coloring extends from just under the gray hooding to a V-shaped point where a yellow vest begins. This yellow continues down the bird's underside to the rump. On mature birds, the charcoal gray is a bit darker than on younger ones. Younger Senegals also have gray eyes that typically transform into a mesmerizing yellow by adulthood. (Interestingly, this is not always the case; my own Senegal's irises haven't even begun to change from their original gray in the decade that I have owned him.)

Males and Females

Some parrot species are sexually dimorphic. This means that males and females are distinguishable by visual comparison. The distinctions are not always obvious, though. Although Senegals are not overtly sexually dimorphic, there are a few subtle ways to tell the difference between the genders.

Male Senegals (cocks) are typically larger and stockier than females (hens). The female's head and beak are also generally smaller and narrower than the male's. Additionally, the vent feathers on a mature Senegal (approximately two to three years of age) are yellow in the male and green in the female. Many owners also insist that the V-shape of the vest on a female Senegal extends lower—all the way down to between the bird's legs, ending instead just midway down the chest on a male.

The only way to be certain that you have correctly sexed your Senegal is by having your avian veterinarian conduct a DNA or surgical test. Although both tests are equally reliable, the former method is considerably safer for the bird. A DNA test entails carefully plucking a small number of feathers (typically between three and five) from the bird's chest. Because it is a tissue sample (not the feathers themselves) that must be examined, feathers falling out natually cannot be used to confirm gender.

Another practical option is requesting a blood test only if your bird must have blood drawn for another reason. Unless you plan to breed your Senegal, whether you have a male or female bird may not matter to you. I have never had any of my own birds sexed, although I did awake to find an egg one morning in what I thought was my male pionus Maximilian's cage.

Meyer's Parrot

A close second in popularity to the Senegal, the Meyer's parrot is actually the most common poicephalus parrot in the wild. Like the Senegal, the Meyer's is greatly admired for his amiable temperament and unique good looks. Primarily brownish gray, the

Meyer's parrots are slightly smaller than Senegals, and they have somewhat calmer temperaments.

Crossbred Poicephalus

One of the most controversial issues concerning parrots is the crossbreeding of two separate species. Allowing parrots of different species to mate often creates more problems than benefits. Many species are simply not capable of producing offspring together—such as a cockatiel and a cockatoo, for instance. More similar species, however, like the nine *Poicephalus*, can procreate together. When this occurs, it is called hybridization, or crossbreeding.

I own a crossbred poicephalus parrot named Jacob. Jake is a beautiful bird with prominent features from both of his parents, a Senegal and a Meyer's parrot. His temperament, though, is another story. He can be enormously sweet at times and he is very smart, but he is also wildly unpredictable and often aggressive. My ten-year-old son isn't allowed to touch him at all yet, and neither my husband nor I allow Jake to perch on our shoulders. We do handle him, but this is a constant work in progress that demands a great deal of patience and a solid training commitment. We accept Jake for who he is, although he may have been more aptly named Jekyl.

I didn't buy Jacob because of his mixed-species status. At the time, I knew next to nothing about this practice. I brought him home because of an immediate connection I felt with him, a bond that I continue to nourish through time and effort and despite painful bites and frustrating setbacks. Certainly, there are many parrots with personalities like Jake's who were not crossbred, and not all hybrids present the same challenges that he does.

Fortunately, Jacob's health has shown no signs of ill effects from his pedigree, but other birds are far less lucky. Because many parrot breeders crossbreed as a means of merely creating rare and enticing aesthetic qualities, health and temperament are often overlooked. If you want to stack the odds in your favor for finding a healthy poicephalus parrot with a pleasing temperament, I recommend avoiding crossbred birds.

Jacob, the author's Senegal-Meyer's hybrid. The results of crossing different species are very unpredictable.

Meyer's parrot can be broken down into six subspecies, each sporting a unique amount of yellow, turquoise, and green feathers on various parts of the body. Because the native habitats of these subspecies overlap to such a great extent, widespread crossbreeding has taken place in the wild. Confusion has also existed among breeders for some time, so this hybridization has undoubtedly continued in captivity. For the sake of simplicity, most Meyer's parrots can be classified as either having yellow on the head or not.

Without an official test, it may be difficult to sex a Meyer's parrot.

Although a male's head and beak tend to be larger than a female's, this can be tough for novice bird owners to distinguish, especially if they have no member of the opposite sex to use as a comparison. The male's head is also said to be flatter on top, but again, this delineation means little without another bird nearby.

The Meyer's parrot usually weighs and measures slightly less than the Senegal parrot—100 to 135 grams in weight and 8 inches (20.3 cm) in length, making it the smallest poicephalus parrot. Some have been said to be as small as 5 inches (12.7 cm) long. This

It is easy to determine the sex of red-bellied parrots; only the male (left) has the namesake red-orange abdomen.

species also inhabits a similar terrain to the Senegal's in the wild, and the parallels do not end there. Like the Senegal, whose eyes turn yellow in adulthood, the Meyer's eyes transition from a deep brown to a fiery red-orange when they reach maturity.

Red-Bellied Parrot

Unlike most of the eight other poicephalus species, the red-bellied parrot is sexually dimorphic. Males have a flaming red-orange chest. All red-bellied babies sport this striking feature, but hens lose their scarlet feathers with their first molt. A few females do retain a bit of their red color, but this is usually minimal, if present at all—and it is greatly overshadowed by the cock's more vibrant red that only intensifies with age. Aside from this one feature for which the species is named, however, male and female red-bellies are very similar in appearance.

Both males and females have bright green underparts, gray wings and head, and piercing red eyes. The beak is black in both sexes. Red-bellies are typically between 9½ and 10 inches (25 cm) in length and generally weigh between 120 and 160 grams once they enter adulthood, a milestone reached between two and four years of age.

Wild red-bellies are found in eastern Africa, including such countries as Tanzania, Kenya, Ethiopia, and Somalia. They are the most common of the five parrot species native to Kenya.

Jardine's parrots are the second largest of the poicephalus, and they can be extremely acrobatic.

Jardine's Parrot

There are three, possibly four, subspecies of the Jardine's parrot. The nominate of these, *Poicephalus gulielmi gulielmi*, is sometimes called the black-winged Jardine. The black-winged Jardine is darker (almost black, thus the nickname) and stockier than the other subspecies. This subspecies also sports a larger beak. The most popular Jardine subspecies here in the United States is the one known as the lesser Jardine, *Poicephalus gulielmi fantiensis*. The lesser Jardine is smaller than all other Jardines, but this subspecies stands out among the rest due to the bright orange coloring on his forehead, crown, thighs, and wing edges. Other Jardines also show a fair amount of this bright color, but theirs falls more within the range of orange-red.

Jardine's parrots typically weigh between 200 and 300 grams and measure approximately 10 to 11 inches (26.65 cm) in length. In the poicephalus family, the Jardine's size is surpassed only by the Cape parrot. In nature, Jardine's parrots are found from western to central Africa, including parts of Uganda, Ghana, Cameroon, Gabon, Tanzania, and Nigeria.

Brown-Headed Parrot

Sometimes called the emerald parrot, the brown-headed parrot can be divided into three subspecies. All brown-heads are primarily green with a brownish-gray head—hence their name. This species is remarkably similar in appearance to the Senegal with the exception that it lacks the colored belly. A brown-head does have yellow under his wings, but this can be difficult to see unless the bird is in flight. Like the Senegal, the brown-headed parrot's iris is yellow, but this is considerably less intense than the Senegal's bright golden color.

Cape Parrot

The Cape parrot offers three subspecies to the poicephalus family. The *Poicephalus robustus robustus*, known as the South African Cape, is the nominate of the three. This bird's neck and head are greenish to yellowish-brown; the body is green.

Brown-headed parrots are found in southeastern Africa, from Kenya to South Africa, along with several nearby islands.

Two subspecies are thought to be a species unto themselves; they are referred to as the un-Cape parrots and known scientifically as *Poicephalus fuscicollis fuscicollis* and *P. f. suahelicus.*

A mature Cape parrot measures approximately 12 inches (30.5 cm) long and can weigh as much as 350 grams. This species is indigenous to South Africa in what are called afromontane forests. These forests are filled with extremely tall trees that these parrots adore.

Ruppell's Parrot
The rarest *Poicephalus* species available for ownership in the United States is the Ruppell's parrot, *Poicephalus ruppellii.* The Ruppell's is most similar in size and shape to the Senegal and Meyer's parrots; most weigh approximately 115 grams and measure 9 inches (22 cm) in length. Its coloring, though, is entirely different from each of its sister species. The Ruppell's body is brownish-gray. Although this species does have bright yellow on its wings like a Meyer's, the Ruppell's does not have any of this color in its head. Still, the yellow is extremely eye-catching due to its stark contrast to the bird's dark feathers. Sexually dimorphic, a female Ruppell's parrot has a blue lower back, abdomen, and rump, whereas the male does not. The beak

The Cape parrot is the largest of the poicephalus. They have a reputation for being sweet and gentle pets.

is grayish black, and the iris is either orange-red or bright red. This species is found in southwest Africa, from Angola to Namibia.

Yellow-Faced Parrot
The yellow-faced parrot is similar in appearance to the Jardine's parrot. Unlike the Jardine's, however, the yellow-faced parrot is a paler green. As this species' name implies, the bird has a large area of yellow on its face and crown, particularly around the eyes.

Wild yellow-faced parrots are found exclusively in Ethiopia in mountain forests. They are not found in US aviculture.

Niam-Niam Parrot

Similar in appearance to the brown-headed parrot, the Niam-Niam parrot, *Poicephalus crassus,* is slightly larger than the brown-head and a bit smaller than the Jardine's parrot. This species has a red iris. The Niam-Niam is found in the moist woodlands of the Central African Republic, Chad, the Democratic Republic of the Congo, and Sudan. There are no subspecies. Like the yellow-faced parrot, the Niam-Niam is not currently bred in captivity in the United States.

Temperament and Behavior

An experienced parrot behavior consultant once told me that she thinks of Senegals as small parrots. "But don't tell the Senegals that," she added quickly, "as they would be very insulted!" This savvy professional with more than 30 years of experience working with birds had summed it up perfectly. Senegals and other poicephalus parrots are truly large parrots in smaller birds' bodies—a fact of which they themselves appear to have no knowledge. They are at once shrewd yet oblivious, gentle yet fearless. Even without the benefit of decades of experience, you will likely notice these qualities in the Senegal after

spending just a short time with one. These expressive birds simply cannot hide their exuberant personalities.

Although poicephalus parrots share many temperamental characteristics, there are a few subtle differences among the species. Senegals are independent thinkers who simultaneously see nothing wrong with taking time out from whatever they are doing for cuddling. Often labeled as clown-like, Senegals delight in making their owners laugh, a common response to seeing these acrobatic little parrots hanging upside down or playing on their backs. When not provided with a constructive means of releasing this entertaining energy, however, a Senegal is doomed to mischief.

Meyer's parrots and brown-headed parrots, on the other hand, are known

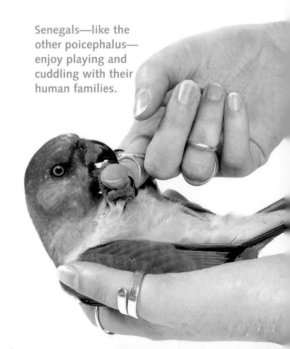

Senegals—like the other poicephalus—enjoy playing and cuddling with their human families.

Are Two Birds Better Than One?

Many people mistakenly assume that parrots kept alone are lonely. Although this may be true when it comes to other animals, it is not the case for most parrots. When cared for properly, a Senegal parrot can be perfectly content being an only bird. Of course, you must make consistent one-on-one time with your bird a top priority, not merely passively spending time with him but enthusiastically interacting with him. Senegals thrive with regular stimulation, and they consider their humans to be vital flock members. If your work keeps you away from home for a considerable part of each day, you may be tempted to provide your Senegal with an avian buddy, but this must be a well-thought-out decision.

If you ultimately decide that your bird does indeed need a friend, select a species that is compatible with your Senegal. In many homes, Senegals coexist with larger parrots such as macaws or cockatoos, but their exchanges are often limited at best. Even smaller species like conures or cockatiels are not guaranteed to get along well with your individual bird. If you choose another poicephalus parrot, the two may safely be allowed to spend time together, but being housed in the same cage will likely lead to the birds bonding with each other more than with you and the rest of your family—or worse, fighting with each other nonstop.

Ask yourself the following questions: Can I give my Senegal the time and attention he needs each day when I am done with work? If so, he will survive being left alone while you are away. Do I know if my Senegal is male or female? If you do not, now is the time to find out with a DNA test because adding a member of the opposite sex to your home may lead to breeding. Most importantly, do I really have the time and resources for another bird? If the answer is no, you owe it to your Senegal (and the hypothetical bird) to wait until your circumstances change to add another pet to your household.

for being significantly calmer than Senegals. They are also clown-like, but their moods are generally more consistent. For this reason, either a Meyer's or brown-head may be a better choice for a family with younger children. Additionally, the Meyer's has a greater potential for bonding closely with more than one person. This species loves meeting new people and exploring new territory, so be sure to latch your bird's cage properly.

Meyer's, red-bellies, and brown-headed parrots all typically enter a nippy phase during the first year after weaning, but this is usually just a brief period. In adulthood, all three species are more prone to shyness than aggression, although red-bellies are also known for being comical show-offs. If speaking potential is important to you, the Senegal, the Cape, and the red-bellied parrot are usually the most proficient in this area.

It's a Guy Thing

Male birds are generally more likely to speak, but this is not a hard and fast rule. If you own both a male and female Senegal, you may likely notice a dramatic difference between the two birds' vocabularies and clarity. If you own only a female, though, you may find your parrot's repertoire to be delightfully extensive. A young hen may sometimes even outtalk many older males. Like people, every parrot is different.

If you own other birds, you may worry about how your new poicephalus parrot will interact with them. Especially if you have larger parrots, like cockatoos or macaws, you might worry that a Senegal would be vulnerable to being bullied by your current flock. Although care must always be taken to protect smaller birds from bigger ones, your Senegal parrot may likely be the more formidable foe, making precaution a two-way street. These little birds have been known to take on birds ten times their size and threaten these more substantial psittacines into surprising submission. What these birds lack in size they definitely make up for in self-confidence.

Their self-assurance can sometimes cause Senegals to instigate the conflicts, though. The Senegal's inclination for gentle human interaction often grows into an especially strong bond between a particular bird and his favorite human. Usually, this just adds to the Senegal's charm, but it can sometimes result in an intense jealousy of other human family members and pets within the household.

Intelligence and Speaking Ability

The first thing most people ask me when they discover that I own parrots is whether they can talk. Talented talkers, the poicephalus parrots not only have a gift for gab, but they also seem to deeply enjoy communicating with their human flock members.

When my family and I head out the door each morning, my own Senegal parrot, MacLeod, almost always offers us a warm "Love ya!" or a hipper "Later, guys!" Is he merely repeating things he has heard each of us say to each other or to him? Surely this is how he learned to say the words and phrases that are part of his extensive vocabulary, but he does indeed seem to know when to use human language in proper context.

One could argue that Mac chooses to bid us farewell when he sees us preparing to depart as a result of conditioning. This is, after all, the setting in which he has heard us use these words many times, and we always welcome his participation in our domestic rituals. Still, there are other phrases that Mac has applied with far less prompting. The best example of this occurred one evening while my husband Scot was away on a business trip. It was the first time he had in fact been away overnight since Mac joined our family. Having heard Scot and I ask each other periodically about the whereabouts of our cocker spaniel, Jonathan, Mac had learned to also ask, "Where's Jonathan?" We had always been impressed with not only Mac's ability to ask this question but also his timing; he never asked the question when Jonathan was within his sight.

On this evening, however, Mac took the inquiry to a new level. He began as usual by asking about Jonathan's whereabouts. I responded by calling my faithful dog, who came trotting

Most Jadine's parrots do not have clear voices, even though they may have a good vocabulary.

into the living room where Mac's cage stood. Mac looked down, bid the dog a quick hello, and then turned his attention back to me. "Where's Scot?" he then demanded. Apparently, I had demonstrated my understanding of his request by producing his friend Jonathan; he now wanted me to deliver his favorite person, Scot.

Mac's articulation certainly isn't as clear as that of an African grey parrot or certain Amazon species. His voice is softer and his vocabulary is surely more limited, but this in no way diminishes his ability to speak to us in a meaningful way. He is forever learning new words and phrases, and he never ceases to amaze me by choosing to use them at precisely the right moments.

At times no words are even required. MacLeod revels in participating in any debate going on within my household, nodding his head emphatically as each family member makes a praiseworthy point during a discussion. We often joke that this gesture is a sign of Mac's endorsement in the argument. Other poicephalus are proficient noisemakers. My Senegal-Meyer's parrot, Jacob, has learned to mimic numerous sounds around our home—including telephone ringtones and microwave beeps—and he always concludes his performance with a hearty laugh when he makes one of us come running to either of these ruses.

As I learned the hard way, poicephalus parrots are also adept escape artists. A few weeks after bringing Jacob home, I nearly began questioning my sanity when I kept returning to the room to find him sitting on top of his cage instead of in it. In the beginning, I would wake to find Jake perched contentedly atop his brass domicile and assume that I had forgotten to close his cage door the previous night. Incidentally, I had been

Watch and Learn

"Do Senegals make good pets for kids?" This is a common question among parents. While Senegals are known worldwide for their friendly nature with both adults and children, the more appropriate question is whether a particular child is kind and mature enough to care for a pet Senegal. Even the most responsible kids are, well, kids.

A parrot must be fed daily, and dishes need to be washed and dried thoroughly before each feeding to prevent the growth of dangerous bacteria. A thorough cage cleaning should be done at least once a week. Although an older child may be trusted to perform these important tasks, an adult must ultimately be responsible for making sure that they are not forgotten.

Younger children will learn from assisting you. They may also be capable of performing fun but less complicated jobs, like picking out new toys or saying goodnight to the bird each evening, and gradually learning how to perform new activities. There is a huge difference between sharing the responsibilities of bird care and leaving a Senegal in the sole care of a child, but carefully involving kids in bird ownership can teach them how to become responsible pet owners themselves when they are ready.

guilty of this dangerous offense with Mac on a few occasions, after which Mac began quietly adjourning to the cage's interior each evening before bedtime came. I will always suspect that he did this to prevent me from noticing my oversight. Unlike Jake, however, Mac had never staged a breakout.

Once I began making a mental note of closing Jake's cage–at times even asking others to witness the task–I finally realized that the only thing I was overlooking was Jake's extraordinary escape skills. For a day or two, I was able to prevent him from escaping by placing a clothespin on the cage's latch, but this additional challenge was also easily overcome. It soon became apparent that the only permanent solution was a door with a more sophisticated handle. To this day I must use two hands to undo the latch on Jake's new cage, but it's a small price to pay for knowing that he is safe when I cannot watch him.

Time and Attention Requirements

Virtually any kind of pet requires a certain amount of time and attention on behalf of his owner. Feeding a bird, keeping his cage clean, and making sure that he gets out of his cage on a regular basis all take up a fair amount of time, but attention goes a bit further than this. Large parrots in particular demand a great deal of one-on-one time with their human family members if they are expected to remain tame and affectionate. The same is true for poicephalus parrots, although the amount of time is far less for these birds than for a cockatoo or African grey, species that are known for being significantly higher-maintenance pets.

Ironically, one of the worst things you can do for a parrot is spend *too* much time with him in the very beginning. Although you certainly want to help your new pet acclimate to his new surroundings, it can actually end up being counterproductive if you don't match the details of this introductory period to your household norms. For example, while it may be advisable to take some time off from work to spend with a new puppy so that you may housetrain him and bond with each other, a parrot will have a harder time adjusting when it is time for you to go back to work. If you spend two weeks at home with him as he gets accustomed to his new environment, he will assume that this is a typical routine, and he will subsequently have to readjust when your vacation time runs out. Instead decide how much time you will be able to spend with your Senegal predictably, and try to be consistent from the very first day. Of course, there will be times when you will have more or less time to spend with your bird, but jumping into your usual schedule with both feet is the best way to make your new Senegal feel right at home.

Suitability as Pets

If you have ever spent time with a large parrot, you know that certain avian species can be extremely loud. I personally think that the term *ear piercing* was invented to describe cockatoos, but loud can sometimes be a relative term. One of the benefits of owning a poicephalus parrot is that in general these charming little birds are delightfully quiet. Of course, they make some noise, but in comparison to other types of parrots, their screeching is typically low in both volume and frequency. Still, this doesn't stop my friend Tom from shuddering nearly every time he enters my home and hears what he considers the shrill cries of my poicephalus parrots. We will often be engaged in a compelling conversation when Tom will start to twitch a bit; it is only then that I realize the birds are making noise at all.

To me the sound of my birds' screams is just the sound of my life—unless, that is, I happen to have a headache. My husband and I agree that we each tolerate the birds' noise level better on some days than others. If I am feeling poorly or trying to concentrate on a project that demands quiet, I too can find my birds to be a bit too loud for comfort. At these infrequent moments, I simply remind myself that it could be a lot worse. They could be cockatoos!

Finding Your Poicephalus

There are many avenues for finding the perfect poicephalus parrot. A quick

Senior Senegals

In the wild, Senegals can live as long as 25 to 30 years, provided that they are able to stay out of the reach of predators. In captivity, Senegals and other poicephalus parrots face different concerns that threaten their longevity. Among these are household dangers such as open doors and windows or standing water like that in sinks and toilet bowls. There are also looming cats and other carnivorous animals, as well as the dangers of certain foods such as chocolate and avocados, which are highly toxic to all birds. The biggest threat to your Senegal's long-term existence, though, is an inferior diet. Poicephalus parrots who are fed seed-only regimens or an excess of human junk food might live to be 15 or even 20 years old if they are lucky, but a Senegal fed a healthy, well-balanced diet has a much greater chance of living up to his potential captive life span of 40 to 50 years or more.

When a particular parrot is considered a senior is similarly dependent on the quality of his care. Senegals who are provided with healthy food, taken for routine veterinary exams, and allowed to exercise regularly will undoubtedly stay youthful and energetic longer than birds who are denied these basic necessities. Make your parrot's overall health a top priority, and you will very likely increase your time together.

Internet search yields dozens of breeders and pet stores in most areas. Visiting them is a great way to learn more about these amazing little birds and just might lead you to the bird of your dreams. Another excellent means of finding a fantastic parrot is through rescue and adoption. Countless birds across the country are in need of new homes, some because their owners didn't take the responsibility of parrot ownership seriously and others because their owners experienced a change in their personal circumstances beyond their control.

Senegal parrots require daily care and interaction with their owners, but they do not need as much attention as some other parrot species.

Of course, some parrots have been neglected or abused to the point where they are less than ideal companions. Sadly, these birds need very special caregivers—those with experience in dealing with chronic behavior problems. Don't assume that every bird in rescue presents this kind of challenge, though. No matter what your experience level, a little legwork can usually lead you to a parrot with needs you can easily meet if you are willing to make the commitment. Think of those rescue workers as people–parrot matchmakers!

2

Senegal Supplies

Before you bring your new pet Senegal home, there are a few things you will need to care for him properly. These items will range in both size and price, but all are important. Careful selection at the outset will save you both time and money in the long run. Some supplies will undoubtedly need replacing from time to time, but the more substantial investments, when sensibly chosen, should last your bird a great many years.

Parrot Provisions

Cage

The most basic item any bird needs is a place to eat and sleep comfortably. For most parrot owners, a cage is the most expensive item they will ever purchase for this purpose. Although a Senegal may certainly enjoy the benefits of a free-flying environment during his waking hours, he may prefer to sleep in closer quarters.

Size and Bar Spacing

The most important factors to consider when shopping for your Senegal's cage are size and bar spacing. The dimensions must allow him to easily spread and flap his wings, as well as move around some. Although a taller cage is a plus, the width of the cage should always be the more important consideration. The minimum measurement for a Cape parrot's cage should be 36 inches wide by 24 inches deep by 36 inches tall (91.4 x 61 x 91.4 cm). The other poicephalus parrots can live comfortably in a slightly smaller cage—no smaller than 24 inches wide x 18 inches deep x 24 inches tall (61 x 46 x 61 cm), but you should always buy your bird the largest cage you can.

Bar spacing should be ¾ inch (about 2 cm). Note that while the recommended cage dimensions are merely a minimum figure, the bar spacing measurement should be as

Buy the largest cage that you can afford for your Senegal, but be sure that there is not too much space between the bars.

Buying a cage with a play gym on top saves you some space and gives your parrot an attractive high spot.

close to exact as possible. If there is a larger space between the bars, your Senegal will be at risk of getting his head or other body parts caught if he tries to squeeze through them. If you must stray from the ¾-inch (2 cm) measurement, go with a narrower spacing, provided the bars are sufficiently strong and secure. Additionally, the cage should be labeled *lead-free* and *zinc-safe*. Brass cages, which can contain zinc, can cause zinc toxicity, so it is especially important that you have it in writing that a cage made from brass is zinc-safe. Stainless steel or powder-coated models are ideal.

Shape

As long as the minimum dimensions are met, a cage may be either rectangular or square, but domed or round cages should be avoided. Like cages with bars placed too far apart, this shape also presents risks of catching wings, toes, or other body parts. In addition to posing physical risks to your bird's health, this shape has also been known to cause psychological problems in some species. Some birds seek out corners when they are feeling insecure; a cage without any right angles leaves a bird like this with no such safe haven.

Horizontal Bars

Another key cage feature is bar orientation. If most of the bars are vertical, this will hamper your Senegal's dexterity considerably. Cross bars are an obvious plus, but an ideal cage will have at least two full sides with the majority of the bars positioned horizontally. Think of these horizontal bars as forming a built-in ladder for your bird, allowing him easy access to his entire cage, literally from top to bottom.

Play Areas

You may select a cage that offers a separate play space on top or one with a ceiling that opens to create such an area. This is not only a great space saver, but it also provides your bird with the opportunity to rise to the highest possible perching spot, an important factor for most avian species that instinctually feel safer at higher elevations.

If you like the idea of a play space but you select an otherwise ideal cage without one, consider investing in a separate play area. One advantage to one of these petite parrot playgrounds, available in both tabletop and freestanding versions, is that your bird can use it virtually anywhere in your home, enabling him to move with you from room to room. A simple T-stand

(a single perch mounted over a tray, often with attached treat cups) can be surprisingly versatile. You can use it either alone or with toys and other treats to provide your Senegal with more time alongside his favorite humans.

Seed Catchers

One feature that will save you cleaning time is a seed catcher. Also called a seed guard, this metal skirting situated at the bottom of some cages helps contain the mess of seeds and other foods, as well as feathers and dander, to the inside of the enclosures. Although an elasticized cloth version may be purchased to cover the bottom section of a cage without this built-in feature, it is vulnerable to the whims of a voracious chewer. I personally also find fabric seed guards to be less effective at ultimately preventing a mess, as they are nearly impossible to remove during cleaning without a fair amount of the debris that they have caught falling onto the floor.

Child Care

Kids can be impressively responsible caregivers for Senegals. Children often develop an easy rapport with these friendly little parrots. Allowing your kids to interact with and care for your Senegal can also be an excellent learning experience for all involved. It is vital, though, that even an extremely mature child not be left with the sole responsibility of a pet. Even if your teenager is capable of all of the necessary tasks, check up on her regularly to make sure that nothing is being forgotten.

Bottom Grill

Sometimes called a grate, a grill sits at the bottom of a cage's interior, placing a barrier between your bird and all of the food and droppings that fall between the bars to the cage floor. Grills are common components to many parrot cages on the market today. Whether you find this item useful may depend on your bird's individual personality and habits. If he likes to shred paper, a grate will be helpful in limiting his access to the cage lining. If your bird is more like my own Senegal, however, you may find that the only time he ventures to the bottom area is when he has dropped something that he wants to retrieve. I have found grills to be more effective at catching droppings than keeping them away from my birds, a downside that echoes on cleaning day. Fortunately, most grills are removable, so you can choose to use one or not.

Wheels

One small but incredibly useful cage feature is the mobility provided by wheels. Whether you are cleaning your bird's cage or you simply want to move it to another part of your home, wheels make any cage portable. As soon as you try to lift a large parrot cage, you immediately understand why many catalog companies charge a premium for shipping these items. This attribute also allows you to place your bird by a window during warmer periods and move him back to his regular position when drafts or cool air is a concern.

Tabletop play stands allow you to take your bird with you as you move about the house.

Cage Placement

Once you have chosen your Senegal's cage, you must then decide which spot in your home is the best location for it. Like many decisions in bird ownership, this one may well depend on the personality of your individual parrot. Oftentimes Senegals love to be in the heart of a home—a living room or family room, for instance—where they will be able to participate in most household activities. Less gregarious birds may prefer quieter locations like dining rooms or home offices.

With a few exceptions, there are no hard and fast rules about where you should and shouldn't place your bird. Beware, however, of placing him in a location that is too remote, such as a bedroom or basement-level room, where your bird might not get enough attention or sufficient natural light. Also, kitchens can be a problematic place to keep a parrot, as certain cooking fumes (particularly those from nonstick pans or from overheated oil) can be lethal to birds. It is also dangerous to allow a bird outside his cage while you are cooking due to the risks posed by boiling water and sizzling foods, as well as the possibility of fire. In general, as long as your bird is not placed in direct sunlight or in a draft, you can place his cage wherever you think he would most like it and where it is convenient for your household.

Microchipping

At one time, tattooing was the most common way of protecting pets against theft. Today, microchipping has surpassed this former identification method in popularity. About the size of a grain of rice, a microchip is inserted under a parrot's skin by means of injection (typically above the breast muscle) and can then be read by a handheld scanner if the bird is recovered after becoming lost or stolen. More and more veterinarians and animal shelters across the country are using microchip scanners as a means of identifying animals, but it is important to note that owners must register their pets' identification number with the microchipping company and keep their contact information current for the chips to effectively serve their purpose.

Have A Safe Trip

Even if you only plan to use it for veterinary visits, a travel cage is a wise investment. Your Senegal's travel cage should provide him with enough room to safely turn around within the enclosure, but he need not be able to spread his wings within it. The door should close securely, as escape is a very real and deadly possibility if it does not. As long as your commute will be a short one, you also needn't provide your bird with food or water for the trip, although a tasty treat will likely be a welcomed diversion for him. If you schedule an exam during a colder month, be sure to place a towel or blanket over your bird's travel cage before heading out—and warm up your vehicle as well. Better yet, schedule routine appointments for a warmer time of the year.

Food and Water Bowls

Food and water bowls typically come with a cage, so this is another feature that should be considered when making a cage selection. How many dishes are there? What material are they made from? How easy is it to remove them from and return them to their holders?

The strongest dishes for parrots are made from stainless steel. You will likely find it convenient if the feeding area of your bird's cage has its own door. This will allow you access to your bird's dishes without having to reach across him or any toys or perches. I also recommend dishes that sit fairly high in your bird's cage, especially if you have dogs.

Avoid most plastic dishes. Your bird might not have a penchant for chewing, but over time, even an occasional chewer will likely show his owner how vulnerable plastic dishes can be to a poicephalus beak. At best this will cost you time and money replacing these ultimately disposable items; at worst it can hurt your bird if he ingests fragments from the dish. Harder plastic dishes may survive the challenge posed by your bird's beak, but check them regularly to make sure that he isn't making a meal of them.

I also recommend purchasing an extra set of bowls for your bird's cage. This will make the feeding process a much more efficient task if you prefer using a dishwasher to washing the bowls by hand. If dishes came with your bird's cage, just ask your retailer about ordering an additional set.

Food cups made of stainless steel are the most durable and easiest to clean.

Toys

To many people, toys are fun and frivolous items. To birds, however, they are serious business. Sure, parrots play with toys, but they also *work* at playing with them. An enormous part of a wild Senegal's day involves foraging for food. This natural instinct on which a wild bird's survival depends is still strong in most domesticated parrot species. Because pet birds spend a great deal of their time inside their cages with their food delivered to them, it is especially important that they have something to do while they are there. Toys that hide special treats and require the bird to maneuver the item a certain way to release the yummy reward are an excellent example of a working bird's toy. Placing nuts still in their shells in one of these toys can lengthen the challenge. Of course, a Senegal's beak is hardly as powerful as a larger species like a macaw, so you may have to get your bird started by cracking just

Like other parrots, Senegals need toys in their cage to prevent boredom, a primary cause of problem behaviors.

a small section of a nut with a harder shell, like an almond or a walnut.

In addition to toys that present parrots with the opportunity to release treats, some toys offer the simple reward of a good time. The importance of more pointless entertainment must also never be overlooked. For example, Senegals adore toys that they can use to make noise. A well-constructed bell may end up being your bird's favorite plaything, but don't stop shopping there. The bird toy aisles of pet supply stores seem to be growing bigger and better all the time with lots of new and interesting choices. A parrot's most acute sense is his eyesight, so look for bright and colorful items that will stimulate his sharp vision.

Although they can be messy and don't last as long as more durable items, lightweight toys your bird can shred will also bring him loads of pleasure. One very popular material for these highly destructive playthings is dried palm leaf, but there are many others too. Some of these toys are even available in convenient rolls, so you can cut off a certain length of the material whenever you feel like indulging your bird in a delightful shred fest. Unfortunately, these toys can cost nearly as much as those with a longer life span, so you must be aware that you are buying highly disposable items.

Always keep at least five different

toys in your bird's cage at any one time, and be sure to rotate them from time to time to keep things interesting. No toy, no matter how colorful or chewable, will hold your bird's attention all day, every day. Remember, when you are bored, you can go out and find new things to entertain yourself. Your Senegal cannot; he depends on you to do his toy shopping for him.

If you have more than one parrot, you may be tempted to rotate toys from one cage to another. As long as your birds are healthy, there may be no harm in this practice, but it is important to note that sharing toys is an efficient means of spreading disease if one bird develops a contagious illness. Even washing the items may not eliminate this risk.

Additionally, some birds form strong attachments to their possessions. My Senegal, MacLeod, values one of his toys—a big ball of twisted rope and rawhide—so much that I don't even remove it when I rotate the rest of his cage toys. This item, which Mac nuzzles up to every night while he sleeps, truly belongs to him. From time to time I have no choice but to remove it briefly for cleaning, but I would never even consider loaning it to either of my other birds.

Perches

Most bird cages come with at least one or two basic dowel-like perches, but your Senegal will need a few additional perches, more if he has a large cage. While traditional wooden perches are completely acceptable, you should also invest in a few other types, each offering your bird a different advantage. The most important factors in the selection of perches are diameter and surface material. It is also vital that all perches be rotated regularly so that your bird isn't spending all his time on any particular kind.

Perhaps the most significant perch in your bird's cage is the one on which he sleeps: his roosting perch. Typically, it is the highest perch in the cage. You will likely notice that your Senegal spends a great deal of his time sitting on this perch both when he is awake and asleep. Make sure that it is the proper size—approximately ¾ to 1 inch (2 to 2.5 cm) in diameter. This will allow your bird to rest comfortably but not hold on so tightly as to cause foot

Natural branches from nontoxic trees are among the best materials to use as parrot perches.

Do Try This at Home

How many of us have looked at the toys in bird catalogs or dangling from the racks of our local pet supply store and said, "I could make that!" after seeing the exorbitant prices for these playthings? Especially if you have more than one bird, paying retail prices for many bird toys can cost a small fortune. You can re-create many of the designs you see for sale for just a fraction of the cost. Be warned, however, that cheaper doesn't necessarily mean easier. I say this as

Making toys for your parrot can help you save money. Some bird owners find this to be an enjoyable activity in its own right.

someone who once went around for an entire week with a thumb inadvertently dyed blue after a toy-making session.

I have found my local unfinished furniture store to be a great resource for thingamabobs and doohickeys for toy-making time because all of the wooden do-it-yourself items (from blocks to balls) in their craft department are untreated and ready for me to morph into my own creations. Craft stores are also excellent outlets for supplies. No matter where you find your materials, though, you must be certain that they are safe for your bird. Pine is both safe and reasonably priced, but it is one of the softest woods. If your Senegal is whittling pine into toothpicks in no time, consider upgrading to oak or another safe hardwood.

Once you have chosen your materials, you will then need to drill holes large enough to accommodate the diameter of your cotton rope. Always use 100 percent cotton, never cotton over nylon. I then use good old-fashioned food coloring (boiling it in the water first works best) to dye the wooden baubles before stringing them together. Other materials that may entice your Senegal include vegetable-dyed rawhide leather and American-made rawhide chews made for dogs. Again, look for untreated items; avoid beef-basted or other flavored varieties. Leather and rawhide serve as resilient chewing surfaces, and they soak up food coloring even better than many kinds of wood.

Although the craft store may sell hardware that you can use to attach your creations to your

Senegal's cage, you may find it less expensive to purchase these items from a hardware store. One thing I have found extremely useful is a package of simple, round key rings. I use C-clamps to attach toys to the cage itself, but the rings serve as effective spacers and make repairing just a section of a damaged toy a breeze.

You are limited only by your imagination. Modeling toys you have seen is a great way to start at this activity, but don't stop there. Design your own one-of-a-kind creations. Also, don't overlook the value of simplicity—a toy need not be elaborate for your bird to enjoy it. Braid the rope, or tie it over and over until you have made a fun ball for your bird to try to untangle. One of my birds' favorite toys is a simple rope-covered metal craft hoop with a diameter slightly longer than the birds' heights.

A great toy for shredding play is a simple paper towel tube cut into short spirals. It is messy once given to the bird but much less expensive than the similarly disposable toys you will find at the pet supply store. Just remember to discard any sections of the tube containing glue before cutting into the tube with your scissors.

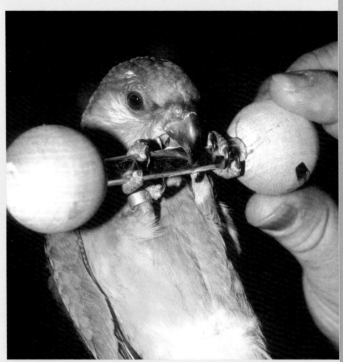

The variety of toys you can make for your parrot is limited only by your imagination.

And don't forget to recycle your bird's old toys when they meet their demise. Sure, the rope and wood might be chewed to oblivion, but save anything else that might be useful for making another toy. I have even found that old dog leashes can be cannibalized to make homemade bird toys. Just cut off the fabric and voilà! You have another great piece of hardware to attach to any toy in your Senegal's cage.

Playing It Safe

Similar to having a small child in the house, owning a parrot means keeping a constant eye on the safety of his surroundings—and I don't mean just his cage. Whenever your Senegal ventures beyond these bars, your casa is his casa, so it is imperative that you make his well-being your top priority no matter where he is. This is an ongoing process; you will continually discover new hazards and need to make adjustments accordingly. Sometimes the necessary changes are minor, but others may be more significant. I remember passing an entire set of high-end cookware on to a family member when my husband and I bought our first parrot and learned that nonstick coatings are harmful to birds. Certain dangers cannot be removed completely, but they can be minimized. Here is a list of just some of the things that can put your bird at risk:

- candles (both the flames and fumes from scents)
- ceiling fans
- chemicals and other toxins (including many household cleaners)
- crushing (by being accidentally sat on by guests or household members)
- electric cords
- hot stovetops
- houseplants (check with your veterinarian for a list of dangerous plants)
- nonstick coatings (used in numerous household items, including pots and pans, irons, ironing board covers, and some hair dryers)
- open windows and doors
- other pets (including cats, dogs, and larger birds)
- self-cleaning ovens (fumes)
- standing water (in sinks, bathtubs, whirlpools, open toilets, and decorative fountains)
- toxic foods (including chocolate, avocados, caffeine, alcohol, and onions)
- suffocation (under blankets and pillows—for example, if your bird is allowed to play near these items)

Remember, nothing takes the place of supervision. Whenever your Senegal is outside his cage, you must be vigilant. When left to their own devices, these curious little parrots can get themselves into trouble in the shake of a tail feather.

problems. The other perches within the cage should vary in diameter and texture.

Conditioning Perches

Conditioning perches (also called grooming perches and therapeutic perches) are made to help keep a parrot's toenails ground down to a healthy length. For this reason, its diameter should be larger than that of your bird's roosting perch so that the nails consistently touch the surface. Conditioning perches are made from a variety of materials, but avoid ones made from cement because they can cause foot injuries.

To ensure that a conditioning perch gets adequate use, you may have to move it from one area to another several times before finding just the right location. A great position is right in front of your bird's dishes, a spot he is sure to occupy several times each day. Once you find an ideal site, you may want to leave this one item in place when rotating the rest of your bird's perches and toys or pick up a few different types of conditioning perches so that even this constant item can be revitalized from time to time.

Natural Wood Perches

One of the best materials for your parrot's perches is natural wood. No, I'm not talking about wood that has been whittled down to look exactly the same as every other smooth rod on the pet supply store shelf. Branches similar to those your Senegal would find in the wild that retain their natural textures and offshoots offer your bird ideal opportunities for foot exercise and comfort. The branch you choose need not be from your parrot's natural habitat to provide these benefits.

One of my favorite types of perching branches is manzanita wood. The branches of this North American tree provide excellent perching areas for Senegals and other small parrots. Apple and lilac branches are also great choices, but be sure that any wood you bring into contact with your bird is free of pesticides and other chemicals. Additionally, any branches you offer your bird should be free of fruit and leaves, which may be toxic even if the wood itself is considered safe.

The best way to ensure that a particular wood is safe is to purchase it from a reputable bird supply retailer. You must also be certain that the wood poses no inherent dangers to your parrot. For example, red maple is highly toxic to birds and should therefore never be used in cages or aviaries. For a complete list of safe and unsafe woods to offer your bird, consult your avian veterinarian.

Rope Perches

Another textured material that offers birds a practical perching surface is rope. Made from braided cotton reinforced by wire, rope perches attach securely to two sides of a cage and can be bent to create different perch formations for your Senegal. If using this type of perch (or any toy made from a material that can unravel), it is important that you keep an eye on the condition of the item. If any threads have begun to loosen, cut them immediately, as they can pose a serious risk of injury to your bird. I learned this the hard way myself when one day I came home to find my Senegal hanging from one wing that had become entangled in a toy with some loose threads I had overlooked that morning. Thankfully, I was able to rescue MacLeod before he suffered any physical injuries from this accident caused by my oversight, but the outcome could have been much worse. More than a decade later, I still feel my heart beat a little faster when I think of this frightening experience from my early days of aviculture. If the loosened threads have compromised the integrity of your bird's perch, remove the structure at once because a fall can also seriously injure a poicephalus parrot.

Plastic Perches

It is imperative that owners understand that perches and toys wear from normal use and that in the case of a bird, normal use often includes avid chewing. For this reason, I highly discourage the use of plastic perches for Senegals. Not only will you likely find yourself replacing these items at a ridiculous rate, but your bird's health could also be compromised by any particles that he ingests during the demolition phase.

Cage Liners

When I was a little girl, my grandparents bought me two parakeets—Pete and Repeat, named after characters from a bedtime story my grandmother used to tell me over and over at my insistence. The birds lived at my grandparents' house in a very 70s-style hanging cage in their dining room. Cleaning this hovering home

Many Senegals enjoy showers, so consider buying a shower perch for your parrot.

appeared to be a simple task. One of my grandparents would simply change the sandpaper-like liner that covered the cage bottom each day. Even at six years old, I could have easily done the job myself had I only been tall enough to reach the tray.

Gravel-Coated Liners

The companies that made this gravel-coated paper (and the gravel-encrusted perch covers that came with it) insisted that these coarse items helped in keeping a bird's nails trimmed down and also that any grit ingested from the material would only help with digestion. Today, many avian veterinarians advise against using grit or gravel-coated liners. Although some smaller species need a tiny amount of grit in their diets to help grind up their food, seed-cracking birds like Senegals and other poicephalus parrots have no dietary need for the substance.

Corncob Bedding

Another popular material for lining cages is corncob. Although it looks attractive and is impressively efficient at absorbing the mess created by spilled water and droppings, this substance can actually kill your bird. When ingested, corncob absorbs the moisture within the bird's body, which can form lethal obstructions. Young birds are also at risk of developing serious infections if they consume the material. If your bird's cage has a metal grate, you may think that this barrier erases the risk, but a curious

and determined bird (which perfectly describes most poicephalus parrots) will find a way to reach it.

Paper

One of the best cage-lining choices is the simplest and least expensive: paper. This conventional material can be layered to help soak up water and other messes. It also makes it much easier for owners to monitor their birds' droppings, an important step in identifying illness.

Most avian veterinarians consider noncolor newspaper to be safe for use in cages. If you prefer to use paper without ink, though, consider purchasing special paper cage liners made to fit the specific measurements of your bird's enclosure. These are available through various pet supply catalogs as well as in many retail stores. You can also use blank newsprint (available at most art and office supply stores) and cut it to fit your bird's cage floor. Another advantage of using any kind of paper is that you can stack it several layers deep and remove only a sheet or two each day for easy cleaning.

Bathing Supplies

Another item that my grandparents purchased for my beloved parakeets was a plastic bird bath that attached to their cage's door opening. I remember filling it with tepid water whenever my grandparents would let me and waiting for what seemed like hours on end for the birds to finally decide that it was time to take a quick dip. This always occurred as soon as I left my vigil, of course.

A rotary tool with a grinding attachment is safer for trimming your parrot's nails than traditional nail clippers.

Senegals also need to bathe regularly, but a portable tub like this is simply too small for them. Instead, you can bathe your poicephalus parrot right in your kitchen sink. All you need is that same lukewarm water I used to run for my parakeets. Soap is not usually necessary and can dry out your bird's feathers and even cause diarrhea (a very dangerous condition for parrots) if ingested. If you use a stopper in the drain to provide your bird with a bath as opposed to a shower, only allow 1 or 2 inches (2.5 to 5.1 cm) of water to accumulate in the basin. Senegals and other members of the poicephalus family cannot swim, and the danger of drowning in even just a small amount of water is very real. This is why you should never leave your bird unattended near water.

If your bird enjoys standing under a cascade of water, consider taking him into the shower or misting him with a spray bottle. Although you may certainly allow him to perch on your hand while in the shower, you may find it extremely helpful to add a shower perch to your bathroom. This convenient device attaches to the interior of your shower wall with suction cups and swings out of the way when not in use.

If you do not provide your Senegal with an opportunity to bathe, he will almost certainly use his water dish as a makeshift bathtub, dousing his cage (and most likely your walls and floor) with his improvised bathwater. This can be frustrating enough if you have just provided your bird with a fresh bowl of drinking water, but it will be even worse when he takes a dunk in water already littered with bits and pieces of his food and other cage debris.

Nail Care

You may prefer to leave the intimidating task of nail trimming to your avian veterinarian, but if you decide to assume this job yourself, you will need either a pair of nail scissors or a rotary tool with a grinding attachment. The latter option is certainly more expensive, but it can be a safer choice because it instantly cauterizes any superficial cuts in the

Have a Game Plan

If you are like most parrot owners, you cannot spend all of your time with your parrot. Does this mean that you should not own a Senegal? Of course not! Your poicephalus parrot will do surprisingly well when left to amuse himself for a few hours at a time, provided that you offer him some stimulating diversions in your absence.

Consider investing in a special group of toys that you offer your Senegal when you cannot be there with him. By placing these items in his cage only when he will be alone, he will positively associate them with times when he must entertain himself. It may take some time to find just the right items that he covets the most; this is largely a matter of trial and error, but as soon as you strike gold, it will be clear. He won't want to relinquish an item he truly loves upon your return, but for the sake of keeping the demand for it high, you must remove it promptly.

Although Senegals aren't excessively noisy by nature, they do love to make a racket with toys with bells and prerecorded sounds. You may find many of these noisemaking toys a little irritating when your bird plays with them over and over (and he will if he likes them), so using these for when you are away is ideal for everyone. If your bird delights in performing as a one-parrot band, however, you may want to allow him at least a few minutes at the end of the day for a private concert.

Another way some bird owners help their Senegals pass their alone time is by leaving the television or radio turned on for them. Although this can be a perfectly harmless form of entertainment, remember to only allow your bird to listen to channels with appropriate content. He may end up repeating anything from obnoxious advertisements to explicit song lyrics. The Senegal's vocabulary is far from that of an African grey or an Amazon, but he can still learn a fair amount of words and phrases—and rest assured, the ones he will end up picking up on his own are the ones you'll wish he hadn't.

nail bed (or quick). No matter which tool you use, always keep a container of styptic powder on hand to speed clotting if needed. This can also be helpful if a blood feather is ever accidentally pulled from your bird.

Cuttlebone

I am always surprised by how many people think that the purpose of cuttlebone is beak sharpening. The truth is that cuttlebone, the calcareous internal shell of cuttlefishes, provides birds with calcium and other important minerals for their diet. The biggest advantage to using cuttlebone instead of trying to provide these minerals in another form is that cuttlebone is completely natural; it contains no toxins or other contaminants as certain manmade mineral blocks often do. Although most parrots will happily gnaw at cuttlebone, don't despair if your Senegal does not. You can simply scrape the cuttlebone into his dish over his food, or you might consider feeding calcium-rich foods like broccoli or brussels sprouts instead.

Cage Cover

I know many bird owners who swear by using cage covers, but I have to confess that I haven't used them for years. My birds maintain a healthy sleep schedule because my husband and I tend to go to bed early most nights ourselves. If you tend to be a night owl

though, you may find that covering your bird's cage with an opaque cloth cover can help him get the rest he needs while you stay up watching the late show each night.

Most parrots need between 12 and 14 hours of sleep nightly. Although your Senegal will nap at odd moments during your waking hours, these intermittent siestas will only count for so much. Nodding off during the day can cost a wild parrot his life, so your Senegal just might nap with one eye open out of a natural instinct to protect himself from predators.

As with toys, a cage cover should be inspected regularly for fraying threads.

A pet carrier makes traveling with your parrot easier.

It is also important that you remember to remove your bird's cover in the morning. Just like sleep, natural light is necessary for parrots. It helps with everything from proper absorption of the nutrients in their food to elevating their mood.

Coming Clean

While a Senegal is far from the messiest bird out there, any poicephalus parrot eats, poops, and molts. The good news is that not everything in your bird's cage needs to be cleaned every day. The bad news is that some of it does. Dishes, for instance, should be washed every time you feed your parrot. Scalding hot water works best. Because most people cannot stand the temperatures necessary to kill bacteria, a dishwasher is a more practical option than heating up tap water. Always allow dishes to dry thoroughly before returning them to your bird's cage.

Toys may also be scalded when they need cleaning. It is a good idea to clean any new toy before allowing your bird to come in contact with it. This is true whether you bought it at a store or ordered it through a catalog because you have no idea how many people touched the item before it came into your possession. If it is a simple toy, dry it with a towel, but if it has multiple surfaces or absorbent sections of rope or other porous material where wetness can lurk, allow it to air-dry before placing it in your bird's cage.

If you change his cage liners daily, you should only need to do a weekly surface cleaning of the cage's interior. Use a pet-friendly cleaner for this task. I like water mixed with a small amount of white vinegar, but safe products are also available at most pet supply stores and other major retailers. Just remember, the label must state that the cleaner is safe for use on animal cages. After removing your bird and his food from the cage's interior, simply spray down all of the surfaces and wipe them with either a clean rag or paper towel. Perches may need to be scraped (with a curved bristle brush) and washed before returning them to their spots.

About three to four times a year, I recommend doing a thorough cleaning on your bird's cage. How you do the cleaning is really a matter of personal preference. I like to take my birds' cages outdoors for a complete dousing with a pressure washer. It's quick, relatively easy, and extremely effective. Other, more patient parrot owners swear by placing their birds' cages right in their showers and using the steam from the hot water to loosen any hardened debris from the bars. Either way is acceptable as long as you use nontoxic cleaners. Diluted bleach, although certainly toxic in its liquid form, is a popular choice because it kills virtually any bacteria with which it comes into contact and is perfectly safe to use provided you allow the cage to dry fully before returning your bird to it.

3

Eating Well

For people, eating a healthy diet means selecting foods that are rich in vitamins and minerals and low in fats and sugars. It also means drinking plenty of water. The nutritional needs of parrots aren't terribly different from this commonsense approach for humans. The best way for people to obtain a variety of nutrients is by eating a variety of foods; this is also the case for parrots. Too much fat, salt, or sugar will cause us to gain unnecessary weight and can place us at greater risk of disease; ditto for our feathered friends. Actually, too much of anything (even a healthy food) is usually a bad thing for both people and animals. When it comes to diet, moderation is crucial.

The basic nutrients your parrot should be getting on a daily basis are water, carbohydrates, proteins, fats (yes, some are good), and certain vitamins and minerals. Even among experts, opinions differ as to exactly which combination of foods makes up an ideal parrot diet. In general, though, fruits, vegetables, nuts, and legumes provide excellent sources of many of these nutrients and should be included in any parrot's diet. Protein and calcium play particularly important roles in the poicephalus parrot's diet, but these nutrients must be offered in the right forms and amounts. If a Senegal isn't getting enough protein, he will eat more than he should in an attempt to fulfill this dietary need,

A poicephalus parrot needs a varied, nutritious diet that includes plenty of fresh fruits and vegetables.

leading him down the path to obesity. If any parrot is given too much protein, though, he could suffer liver damage. The brown-headed parrot has been said to be at particular risk of a serious condition called fatty liver syndrome when fed too much fat or protein. The avian body isn't designed for digesting dairy products, so it is helpful to know that dark green leafy vegetables are excellent sources of calcium, as are soy products.

Sprouted seed is more nutritious than dry seed.

The Diet of a Wild Bird

Being a bird of open woodland and savannah, the wild Senegal is considered a pest to neighboring farmers, whose crops he regularly feasts upon whenever the opportunity arises. The most common foods Senegals partake of in their natural habitat are fruits and blossoms, but these little parrots are very open-minded in their opportunism. They will also readily munch on vegetables, seeds, nuts, grains, and beans.

Many aviculturists think that this wild diet of natural foods is best for pet poicephalus. This is true to a certain degree. Perhaps a more realistic goal is to use the wild bird's diet as a guide for feeding your pet Senegal. After all, tracking down the seeds of locust beans (a wild Senegal favorite) may be a bit of a challenge on this side of the Atlantic Ocean, but garbanzo beans (also known as chickpeas) offer similar nutrients and can be found in most American supermarkets.

Birdseed

Why It's not a Complete Diet

Most parrots love seeds. In addition to being tasty, many seeds offer vitamins such as niacin and riboflavin, as well as essential amino acids and minerals. Sprouted seeds are best because their chemical composition affords them an ideal amount of proteins and essential fatty acids. Unfortunately, nonsprouted seeds contain fatty oils that fall short of this healthful property. Owners must also follow instructions carefully to prevent harmful bacteria from developing while soaking seeds.

Sunflower seeds, an eternal favorite among parrots, are made up of nearly 50 percent fat and should therefore be

Paula Wanna Feed Polly a Cracker?

If your child wants to help feed your Senegal, let her! No matter how old she is, there is something she can do to help at feeding time. My ten-year-old son rushes home from school every day anxious to help me feed our birds. His primary job is to measure out the pellets and seeds, but I also let him help choose which other foods to offer so that we are constantly offering a good variety of nutrients. During this process he has learned a great deal about healthy eating himself. It has also taught him what is and isn't acceptable to offer the birds. Older kids can be responsible for making sure that a bird always has clean water, slicing fruits and vegetables, or even cooking for your Senegal. One of the easiest foods to prepare, whole-grain pasta, is one of my birds' favorite entrees.

limited. Some birds enjoy this type of seed so much that they will refuse to eat almost anything else unless their owners take a stand on this important issue. For a parrot already accustomed to eating an all-seed diet, this may mean that the owner must remove sunflower seeds from the parrot's diet for a stint, adding them back into the regimen in more conservative amounts as the bird acclimates to a new, healthier plan. This can be a tricky process, as parrots are stubborn creatures, and you must be certain that your Senegal is indeed eating enough of his other food once this highly coveted item has been eliminated.

The problem with seeds emerges when they are overused. No food can be relied upon as an exclusive source of all of the nutrients a parrot needs–not seeds, not pellets, nor any one fruit or vegetable. The danger in feeding seeds is when one *only* feeds seeds. Even

offering a variety of seeds by themselves will leave your bird nutritionally deficient and at greater risk of illness– and ultimately a shorter life span.

Even if you are supplementing the seeds with a host of other nutritious foods, your Senegal won't know when to say when to the seed portion of his meal. He will fill up on those yummy fats and barely touch the other nutritious foods that his body so dearly needs. So seeds should be the supplement, not the other way around.

Spotting Bad Seed

Another important consideration when feeding seeds is freshness. I used to purchase all of my bird food from a quirky older woman who ran a small parrot supply store about 15 miles (24.1 km) from my home. Certainly, it would have been easier for me to make the shorter trek to a larger retailer, but I truly enjoyed speaking with this experienced aviculturist. I remember asking her during one such visit what the shelf life of a particular food was. I wanted just a small amount of these particular pellets, but she only had 40-pound (18.1-kg) bags on the shelf. She replied not by scanning the package's label but by opening the bag and tossing a few of the pellets into her mouth as she explained that she would sell me whatever amount I wanted. My first reaction was to blurt out, "Oh, you don't have to check it yourself!" But she wasn't the least bit taken aback by my comment. She merely giggled and said, "Honey, I won't feed my birds anything I'm not willing to sample myself. By the way, this stuff should stay fresh for you in a closed container whether you take the whole bag or just some of it. And if you're still concerned, you can always toss it in the freezer." I bought my supplies from this woman until she retired and closed her shop.

For the sake of your dental health, I don't recommend tossing seeds into your mouth to check their freshness. Instead, rely on your other senses. Fresh seeds are shiny and free of dust and do not have a strong odor. Spoiled seeds smell musty. It is especially important that fresh seeds be kept in an airtight container to keep them fresh. Mildew can develop quickly if seeds are left exposed to air and the moisture within, and this can be lethal to your bird. Also, toss any seeds that are clumped or contain cobweb-like threads, as these are signs of insect infestation.

You should also make a habit of purchasing moderate amounts of seeds rather than stocking up on this item. Although seeds can be stored safely in either the refrigerator or freezer, important vitamins are lost during storage, and this nutritional decline isn't apparent upon visual inspection of the food. Because your parrot should only be eating a small amount, it is especially important that the seeds he

Feed your Senegal seeds in moderation; although seeds are good sources of some nutrients, they are high in fat.

does get retain as many nutrients as possible.

How Much Seed to Include in the Diet

Seeds should only make up approximately 10 percent of your Senegal's diet. Because this minute amount can be difficult to measure out into a daily serving, consider only feeding seeds on certain days of the week. Feeding larger amounts can even have a negative impact on how your bird processes his nutrients. Calcium, for instance, must be properly balanced with phosphorus in the avian body

Try and Try Again

The first time I offered my Senegal-Meyer's parrot, Jacob, a cucumber, he instantly dropped it on his cage floor. The second time he did the same thing. Even after the third and fourth attempt, he still wasn't biting—literally. Jake is my picky eater, always skeptical of any new food item I give him. I have learned that persistence does pay off with him, though. By the fifth time I placed a piece of cucumber in his dish, he picked it up and ate half of it right away. Cukes still aren't the first veggies he reaches for, but he is willing to eat at least a small amount of them. If I had given up after a single try (or even after several tries), I never would have discovered this.

for optimum health. The low ratio of calcium to phosphorus in seeds makes calcium deficiency a greater risk for birds who are overfed seeds.

Pelleted Foods

Few issues elicit such passionate disagreement among parrot owners as whether pellets offer the best nutrition for pet birds. Some feel that sound nutrition cannot be achieved through so-called one-stop shopping. In other words, no one food can provide a bird with all of the nutrients his body needs. This is certainly true, but it is important to note that most avian veterinarians and breeders who support this feeding method recommend offering a pellet-*based* diet, not pellets alone. A general guideline is 75 to 80 percent pellets with the remaining foods consisting of fruits, vegetables, complex carbohydrates, and proteins. Other owners fear that the chemicals used to provide pellets with a reasonable shelf life place their birds' health at risk. This too is certainly a legitimate concern, which is why it is so important to read labels and understand what all of those polysyllabic words mean.

Pros and Cons

Obviously, one of the biggest advantages to using pellets is convenience. Few parrot owners have comprehensive knowledge about avian nutrition. Even if they had the time and money to fill their fridges with everything their parrots' bodies require, most owners would find meeting all of their birds' dietary needs to be an enormous challenge. Sure, most owners can tell you that carrots are healthier than carrot cake, but how many know exactly how much beta-carotene a Senegal should be getting each day? And which is a better source of both beta-carotene and vitamin C–those carrots or sweet potatoes? Reputable pellet companies have made knowing the answers to these questions their business. (Incidentally, the answer is sweet potatoes.)

Another advantage to feeding pellets is the reassurance that your bird is actually getting all of the vitamins you are putting before him. I know that my parrots will each pick out their favorite foods when I serve them their fresh fruits and veggies. This means that they are each getting a slightly different amount of important vitamins and minerals from fresh foods. By feeding my birds a pelleted diet, I know that any holes in either my menus or their eating habits aren't

If you feed your Senegal pellets, choose the one with the fewest preservatives and the greatest number of natural ingredients you can find.

causing nutritional deficiencies.

Spoilage is also a factor when considering a pelleted plan. Unless you shop daily, you may find it nearly impossible to keep a constant supply of all of the fresh foods your bird needs without wasting a large percentage of your investment. Most pellets, however, can be stored for at least a month in a sealed package and longer if they are kept in the freezer.

Critics of pellets point out that eating these homogeneous pieces of kibble-like food is unnatural for parrots. They also worry that the innate nutritional value of many of the ingredients in pellets is lost in the high temperatures of the manufacturing process. To compensate for this, pellet companies incorporate supplements to replenish any lost vitamins, but as pellet opponents argue, vitamins are best served as part of the foods that naturally contain them.

Smart Snacking

When we want to treat our birds, it's easy to reach for the obvious—yummy foods that we don't offer our pets every day, like a potato chip or a piece of a doughnut. Indulging in these less healthy treats once in a while probably won't hurt our birds. There are, however, better ways to treat our beloved parrots. Because I feed my birds fresh fruits and veggies daily, I sometimes see foods like pineapples and cucumbers as the ho-hum staples of their diets, certainly nothing out of the ordinary. So when I want to spoil my birds, these foods don't instantly spring to mind. For my Senegal parrot MacLeod, though, a piece of pineapple is like a slice of heaven. I may not consider it a treat, but he sure does.

If you want to give your Senegal something really special, consider the foods he loves but you simply do not feed as often because they are excessively messy. In our house, these are fresh strawberries. All of my birds adore them, but I'm not crazy about cleaning their staining residue off perches or a spattered wall. For this reason, strawberries provide an excellent opportunity for me to treat my birds when the mood strikes—and when it's my husband's turn to clean cages! Perhaps the object of your parrot's culinary affection is expensive, an exotic fruit that has a short shelf life, which is why you don't offer it daily or weekly. It doesn't have to stain your wall or break your budget to be special, though. You can pick any food you know your bird likes and only offer it as a treat or a reward in training.

If you are offering junk food as treats, remember to limit both the amount and frequency. When your parrot eats just one potato chip, he is consuming the equivalent of an entire bag for a person. Indulge him wisely, and remember that treats don't have to be edible. A new toy or a trip to a room in your home he rarely gets to visit may fill your bird with more excitement than a mere snack cake ever could.

Qualities of a Good Pelleted Diet

Just like other types of commercial pet foods, bird pellets are not all created equal. For your Senegal to enjoy the benefits a prepackaged diet can offer, you must select a brand that is nutritionally sound and free of harmful preservatives and other chemicals. It is also wise to select a variety made specifically for African species, whose dietary needs differ somewhat from those of parrots from other parts of the world.

Millet spray is a treat that most Senegals and other poicephalus enjoy.

Although virtually any prepackaged food must contain some type of preservative to keep it fresh, some alternatives are safer than others. Bird pellets containing tocopherols, antioxidants that retard oxidation to keep foods fresh, are ideal.

Synthetic preservatives are another story. Butylated hydroxyanisole (BHA) and butylated hydroxytoluene (BHT) have come under particular scrutiny in recent years. Studies of BHA and BHT have revealed that high levels of these preservatives can cause tumors in the forestomachs of rats, mice, and hamsters. Because there hasn't been adequate research in animals lacking forestomachs, though, the Food and Drug Administration (FDA) currently allows the use of these preservatives in most pet foods. Although the amount of food a parrot consumes may be considered small, remember that your Senegal's diminutive size means that these questionable chemicals may affect him even more quickly than other animals.

Ethoxyquin, although technically an antioxidant, is another common preservative that has raised many eyebrows in the pet food industry. Fewer studies have been conducted on this preservative, so you will likely see more of it among the ingredients of various kinds of bird food. However, there has been sufficient concern for the FDA to request that pet food manufacturers lower the levels of this ingredient in their products. In addition to being used in some pellet varieties, ethoxyquin is also used in many different bird treats.

There is an ongoing debate among aviculturists about whether propylene glycol is safe. The FDA's official position on this organic compound used as a solvent for food colorings and flavorings is that it is "generally recognized as safe." It is important to note, however, that propylene glycol is also used for an amazing number of nondietary products. These include cosmetics such as baby wipes and shampoos, certain types of automobile antifreeze and brake fluids, and even paintballs for the sport of the same name. Because it tastes extremely sweet, propylene glycol is a clever ingredient for pet food companies to use in their products, but your bird might be better off if you choose foods that do not contain this unusual ingredient, which is strong enough to dissolve the barnacles off a boat.

Fruits and Vegetables

Why Feed Them

One of my favorite things about being a parrot owner is sharing the healthy food I eat with my birds. Be it my morning fruit and cereal or the salad and bread I have with my dinner, nearly any food that I eat regularly myself can safely go into my Senegal's dishes. In addition to being fun—you haven't lived until you've watched an 8-inch (20.3-cm) parrot hold a thinly sliced pineapple ring—the benefits of feeding your bird fresh fruits and vegetables are numerous. Although pellets lay a practical foundation for your parrot's diet, commercialized foods lack phytonutrients, nutritionally important compounds found only in plants. Fruits and vegetables also contain a significant amount of water, helping to keep a bird properly hydrated.

Nuts are high in fat, so feed them in small quantities or as treats.

Senegal Parrots

Feeding fresh foods provides your bird with a variety of tastes and nutrients without the unnecessary additions of salt, sugar, and preservatives. Even shopping for new fruits and vegetables to try can be fun. Have you ever eaten a prickly pear? How about dragon fruit?

Good Choices

Most foods are best when left raw, but carrots provide optimum benefits when slightly steamed, which allows their beta-carotene to be properly assimilated by the bird. Dark, leafy green vegetables like broccoli, kale, and spinach are excellent sources of vitamin K, iron, and calcium. Jardine's parrots in particular are said to need higher amounts of dark orange and green vegetables. Other smart vegetable choices are sweet potatoes, squash, eggplant, romaine lettuce, peppers, and green beans. In general, the darker the color of a particular fruit or vegetable, the more nutritious it is. Wheatgrass is also an extremely nutrient-rich veggie.

Common fruit choices include apples, oranges, and grapes, but more exotic varieties such as papayas, kiwis, and pomegranates provide similar amounts of important vitamins like A, B, and C and can be found at most large grocery stores. Be sure to remove any pits or cores before feeding, though, as these can be toxic. Apple seeds should also never be left inside the fruit because they contain a cyanide compound. Grape seeds, on the other

hand, are completely safe. If you are unsure if a particular type of seed is acceptable, the best approach is to err on the side of caution and remove it.

How to Prepare

Some fresh foods require virtually no preparation on your part, but the first step should always be washing any fruit or vegetable that you won't be peeling prior to feeding because the skins often contain pesticides. Unfortunately, most of the vitamin C in fruits is found in the skin, so buying organic fruits is preferable to peeling. When I'm in a hurry, I always reach for bananas when selecting a fresh food for my birds. I have also found that tangerines are a lot easier and quicker to peel than oranges when time is a factor. Due to their waxy skins, regular cucumbers are never given in my home without first being peeled. If you like the idea of adding a little extra fiber to your Senegal's diet, consider feeding unpeeled European cucumbers–they lack this waxy exterior. Fiber, a beneficial part of a human diet, has not been proven to be necessary for parrots, but it is certainly not harmful and may possibly be useful to them as well.

Once you have washed your produce, simply slice it into sections your parrot can easily handle. I mentioned feeding pineapple rings earlier. It is fine to serve your Senegal larger sections of foods like these as long as they are sliced into thin, lightweight pieces that he can hold. Experimenting with size and shape is

Foods to Avoid

Parrots can safely enjoy so many of the same foods that we humans do that it's often easy to overlook the foods from our healthy diets that can harm our birds. The best rule is to always check with your avian veterinarian before introducing a new food. This is especially important with all of the exotic fruits and vegetables now available in most grocery stores.

Until a recent visit to a Chinese restaurant, I didn't even know what longan fruit was, never mind whether it was safe to share with my birds. (It is when peeled and the seeds are removed.) Avocados, on the other hand, are unsafe for any parrot but particularly African species, so never give your Senegal guacamole.

Here is a list of some common human foods you should never give your parrot:

Never give your bird...	Because...
Alcohol	A bird's liver cannot metabolize alcohol.
Avocados	This fruit is highly toxic to parrots, especially African species.
Caffeine	This alkaloid found in coffee, tea, and numerous soft drinks damages a bird's central nervous system and kidneys.
Chocolate	Containing a substance called theobromine, chocolate poses similar risks to parrots as caffeine.
Dairy products, such as milk, cheese, and yogurt	Birds lack the enzyme necessary for digesting lactose.
Junk foods, particularly sugary or salty snacks	Empty calories from sugar contribute to obesity. Too much salt can cause hypertension and cardiac failure.
Kidney beans and lima beans (uncooked)	When served raw, these beans can be toxic, causing digestive upset.
Melted cheese	Although all dairy products should be avoided, melted cheese (like that on pizza) is especially dangerous, as it poses a choking hazard to parrots.
Onions and garlic	They can cause kidney problems and blood-cell problems.

another way to add fun and variety to your bird's meals. I find that my birds enjoy eating cucumber sticks much more than cucumber slices, likely because they can hold onto them better.

Remember, feeding fresh foods means shopping in the produce section. Canned or dried fruits and vegetables are laden with sugar and sodium. If you like the idea of keeping some easy-to-feed fruits and veggies on hand that won't spoil quickly, consider investing in a food dehydrator. Dried foods are fine—it's that darn sugar that makes the prepackaged ones unhealthy. I regularly dry apples, oranges, bananas, and pineapples for my birds (and even snack on some of them myself). Foods with exceptionally high water content (such as watermelon) aren't recommended for drying, though. I have also found that smaller fruits like raspberries and blueberries virtually disappear during dehydration, making just a small container a rather expensive endeavor.

No-salt whole-grain crackers are healthy treats for poicephalus parrots.

Other Human Foods

Because parrots are considered lactose intolerant, it is not a good idea to offer your Senegal milk or cheese. There are, however, some excellent soy-based alternatives to most dairy products. Another human food you can give your birds is whole-grain bread or other complex carbohydrates. My flock loves oatmeal, but I try to steer clear of most flavored varieties. If you think that plain oatmeal tastes too bland, add some cinnamon but skip the sugar. Instant oatmeal is fine as long as you make it with water instead of milk. You can also serve it uncooked. Never give your bird any food that has just come off the stove or out of the oven or microwave or directly from the refrigerator. Food is best served to parrots at room temperature.

Pet parrots need a smaller amount of carbohydrates in their diets than their wild contemporaries because they do not spend as much time flying and foraging for food. Still, carbohydrates can help provide your Senegal with the energy he needs to carry out his daily activities. The key is to avoid simple sugars and starches, such as white breads and white potatoes.

Continuing to introduce your parrot to different foods will teach him that trying new things can be fun. Just like people, birds have different personalities. Some can become set in their ways and end up extremely resistant to change unless their owners make it a regular part of their routine.

A new food can also be a great motivator for training.

Good Choices

Parrots are herbivores, meaning they primarily eat plants. Although a small amount of low-fat meat, such as chicken, won't hurt your bird, many owners find the idea of feeding poultry to parrots disturbing. Others don't seem to be bothered by it at all. A good friend of mine prepares his poicephalus parrot a dish of his own every Thanksgiving, complete with a tiny serving of turkey alongside his cranberry sauce. My husband, on the other hand, has made me promise never to do this for our birds.

Healthy human food options include whole-grain pasta (either cooked or uncooked), brown rice (cooked only), whole-grain breads, low-sugar cereals, and low-salt crackers. Thoroughly cooked eggs (hard boiled or scrambled, for instance) may be offered occasionally but shouldn't be fed too often due to their high cholesterol content.

Feeding Schedule

Feed your Senegal every day. Throw away any leftover food from the previous day, and wash his dishes thoroughly before returning them to his cage refilled. You should be tossing a small amount of pellets out each time because pellets and fresh water should be available to him at all times. A practical guideline is to feed slightly more pellets than your parrot will eat in a 24-hour period. Perishable foods and seeds should be given at the same time every day and subsequently removed from the cage about an hour or two later to prevent spoilage.

Most foods that are healthy for you are healthy for your parrot. However, it's best not to assume what's good for you is also good for him.

When deciding whether to share foods with your Senegal, ask yourself this question: Is this food healthy for me? If the answer is no, it will almost certainly be a bad idea for your bird.

Supplements

Although certain vitamin supplements may be useful to parrots with specific health concerns, most poicephalus parrots eating well-balanced diets do not require the addition of these trendy substances to their feeding regimens. On the contrary, offering supplements without doing thorough research beforehand can adversely affect a parrot's health.

The best way to provide your Senegal with good health is to feed foods rich in healthful properties. Granola, for instance, is a great addition to the poicephalus diet. It consists of various kinds of oats, fruits, and nuts–foods naturally rich in vitamins and protein. Beware of granola bars, though. Many of these compressed snacks have much more in common with candy bars than their healthy sounding names imply.

Flaxseed, another healthful food, offers numerous advantages to a bird's health due to its inherent ability to balance omega-3 and omega-6 fatty acids in the body. Low levels of omega-6 fatty acids have been linked to decreased serotonin levels in the brain, which in turn can result in depression and related behavioral issues such as feather plucking. With an appealing nutty flavor, flaxseed is an ideal way to treat your bird and naturally supplement his diet.

Water

The most overlooked nutrient, water is an essential part of your Senegal's diet. In addition to keeping him hydrated, this basic liquid is what transports nutrients throughout his body and helps remove wastes in the form of excrement. Just as water supports your human body, it helps regulate your Senegal's body temperature and makes good circulation and digestion possible.

Because most parrots enjoy soaking certain foods in their water before eating them, a bird's water dish can be a breeding ground for bacteria. For this reason, it is paramount that you change your Senegal's water dish at least once every day, thoroughly washing it before refilling it and returning it to his cage. Your bird's cage is essentially his dining room, living room, and bathroom all at once, so it is also important that you change the water immediately if you notice any fecal matter floating in his bowl. Sometimes a simple re-evaluation of perch placement can make this unpleasant occurrence happen less frequently.

If your Senegal makes gazpacho out of any meal you put before him or if he has a tendency to bathe in clean water as soon as it's placed in his cage, consider investing in a water bottle instead of using a conventional bowl for his drinking water. Purchase a glass water bottle, not plastic, or you will find yourself replacing it almost right away, not to mention mopping up the contents. Pet supply stores make glass bottles especially for birds of all sizes. Unlike a rabbit or guinea pig's water bottle, however, your Senegal's will be outfitted with a metal hanger that you must securely install in his cage (typically with a screwdriver) to prevent

Leading a Bird to Water

Senegals are extremely smart birds, but you must never expect your bird to learn something without being taught. If you add a water bottle to his cage, be certain that he knows how to use it before you start using his old water bowl as an extra food dish. Your bird will likely investigate the bottle as soon as you install it in his cage. He may even think that it's a new toy. Take advantage of this opportunity by showing him how water is released when the ball bearing is touched. Because some water will leak from the bottle on its own, you mustn't rely on water level alone as an indicator that your bird has caught on. Don't remove his water bowl from the cage until you actually see him drinking from the bottle. It may take him just a minute or two to master this milestone, or it could take a week or more.

Like other parrots, Senegals seem to prefer their food in easily manipulated pieces.

the glass from falling and breaking. Bring along the dimensions of your bird's cage when shopping for this item because the structure's height and bar spacing measurements will help determine which bottle you'll need.

Monitor the bottle carefully to be certain that your Senegal is able to drink from it. The ball bearing at the end of the delivery tube should move easily when touched lightly. Senegals are like mischievous toddlers—many have been known to wedge objects into this area, effectively preventing the flow of drinking water.

Finally, never let your bird's water dish or bottle become dry. This is just as important as not letting his water become contaminated. Liquid evaporates even in cold weather, but it is particularly important to monitor your bird's water during warmer months. Lack of water (whether by way of owner neglect or a faulty water bottle) can prove fatal to a bird in just a few days.

4

Good Grooming

You certainly won't spend hours on end coifing your Senegal's feathers as you might a Cocker Spaniel's coat or a Persian cat's fur, but there are a few things that must be attended to regularly if you want to keep him looking and feeling his best. He will take on his fair share of these responsibilities, but even with a parrot, self-grooming can only accomplish so much. Owners must also do their part.

Bathing

One of the easiest ways to keep your bird clean is to bathe him weekly. If your Senegal is particularly fond of water, bathing him more often is fine. Some birds enjoy being misted with a spray bottle, while others prefer a shower or bath. If you mist your bird, never use a bottle unless you are absolutely certain that it has never contained chemicals of any kind. Also, no matter which form of bathing your bird likes best, never leave him unsupervised near water. Parrots cannot swim and can drown in even a tiny amount of standing water. Another smart safety measure is to use a rubber mat if bathing your bird in a sink to protect him from slipping. Unless he has gotten oil (or another potentially dangerous substance) on his feathers, it is best to avoid the soap and bathe your Senegal in the simplest and most practical medium: water.

Use water that feels warm (but not hot) to you, and be sure that the water pressure isn't too harsh for this small creature. Always use a towel to gently pat your parrot dry once his shower or bath is complete. In the winter months, consider turning up the heat until his feathers have completely air-dried. There is no need to use a hairdryer on your parrot; in fact, the nonstick coatings on the heating coils of many

Senegal parrot after a bath. Most poicephalus enjoy getting wet.

dryers can produce fumes that are lethal to birds. Plan baths for daytime hours, and if the weather is extremely cold, postpone bathing until the temperature rises.

You may find it convenient to bring your Senegal parrot into the shower with you. Consider wearing a T-shirt to protect your skin from his claws if he flails about when you close the shower door or curtain. All three of my birds enjoy showering, but Jake in particular finds it to be a fun activity. I always position the shower perch so that he can easily walk away from the cascading water if he chooses, but it's always the wet end of the perch he claims.

The use of a nail file will help prevent your parrot's nails from overgrowing, but they will still need occasional trimming.

Finally, pay attention to your bird's reactions to bathing. If he becomes upset when you mist him, don't do it! There is no rule that states that a parrot must be bathed any particular way. Some parrots love to roll around in a shallow amount of water in the sink but detest the feeling of water falling onto them from above. If this sounds familiar, save your bird the stress of a shower. Likewise, if your Senegal seems indifferent to a bath but sings in the shower like Jake, go that route instead. If your bird is among the few parrots who don't appear to enjoy bathing whatsoever, limit baths to the

minimum frequency of once per week, and make them as short as possible. You mustn't skip the process altogether, though, as feathers often become dry and itchy without bathing, a situation that can lead to plucking.

Nail Care

Just like other animals, parrots have toenails that are constantly growing. Allowing them to get too long can cause your bird to injure both himself and others, as well as prevent him from perching correctly, a situation that can lead to painful foot problems. Although the use of conditioning perches helps keep a bird's nails ground down, trimming will still be necessary from time to time. If you have forged a trusting relationship with your poicephalus parrot, he may allow

Children Can Help With Grooming— no Kidding!

The most practical grooming task to encourage children to help with is bathing your Senegal parrot. Clipping nails and trimming wings can be overwhelming tasks even for experienced adults, but bathing—when properly supervised by a grown-up—is an important yet extremely kid-friendly activity. Younger children can easily handle a misting bottle; older kids can help you bathe your bird in a sink or shower. Toddlers can even be made to feel part of the process by simply being allowed to watch while you bathe your parrot.

you to use an emery board to reduce the length of his nails when necessary. Many birds will resist this procedure, however. This leaves you with two options: trimming the nails yourself or deferring the task to a professional. If you prefer the latter choice, you are not alone. Many owners simply do not feel confident enough that they will remove just the right amount of the nail; some would rather take on virtually any other responsibility than risk harming their bird. If you find yourself hyperventilating just reading this, rest assured that you will be doing the right thing by erring on the side of caution.

If you want to try handling your Senegal's pedicure yourself, there are a couple of things you should know before beginning. First, always wrap your bird in a towel when trimming nails. This will enable you to hold him securely and prevent you from hurting him accidentally. It will also help protect your hands if he tries to

bite you. Second, have styptic power or another coagulating agent on hand. Sold at most pet supply stores, this product will be necessary if you accidentally nip the quick, a small vein inside the nail that is nearly impossible to see from the outside.

The best device for safely trimming a Senegal's toenails is a rotary grinding tool (particularly a cordless version). This handheld unit can be affixed with a grinding stone attachment. The grinding tool produces enough heat to instantly cauterize a wound if you accidentally remove too much of your bird's toenail. Extreme caution must still be used, of course, but many parrot owners find this method less intimidating than using nail scissors.

Holding your parrot's foot gently but securely between your thumb and forefinger, apply the rotating stone to the tip of his nails one at a time. (If using scissors, snip just the end of the nail.) It is always better to remove too little than too much, as you can go back later to finish the job if needed, but you can never reattach what you have trimmed away. If you are unsure whether you have removed enough of the nail, watch your bird's foot as he stands on a level surface. The nail should not raise the ball under the end of the toe off the surface on which he stands.

If you inadvertently cut into the quick, apply styptic powder to the area immediately. If bleeding persists, seek veterinary attention. In a pinch, you can use cornstarch, soap, or a wet tea bag as a coagulant. If you find yourself reaching for the clotting agents too often, though, this may be a sign that this task is better left to a professional or that you simply need some hands-on training.

A great way to learn how to trim your Senegal's nails is by watching your veterinarian perform the task. Ask her to demonstrate a nail trim and then to supervise you as you attempt it yourself. If you have any questions about nail trimming, this is an ideal time to ask them.

Beak Care

If you provide your bird with adequate chewing opportunities, beak trimming should only be needed periodically, if at all. Soft wood toys, nuts, and sugarcane are all very practical chewable items that can help keep your Senegal's beak in perfect condition– smooth, shiny, and only moderately long. Climbing, playing, and eating

also help in this process. If you notice that your bird's beak is excessively long or flaked, ask your veterinarian to take a look, as these can sometimes be signs of ill health. Once your vet has ruled out illness, she may suggest just grinding the beak down a bit to keep it in proper shape. An excessively long beak can interfere with eating and self-grooming.

Done with a rotary tool, file, or human fingernail clippers, beak trimming is similar to nail trimming in many ways. Perhaps the biggest similarity to nail trimming is the importance of learning how to perform this task correctly before attempting to do it on your own. In fact it is even more crucial that this grooming job be done by a well-trained individual, as a botched trim can make it difficult or even impossible for a bird to eat.

I prefer to leave this task to the more capable hands of my veterinarian. Because the effects of a mishap could be both permanent and devastating, I am simply not comfortable performing this task.

Wing Clipping

For millions of years, what has set birds apart the most from other animals is their remarkable ability to fly. Nothing is more natural to a bird than using his wings to lift himself into the air and soar freely as nature intended. In the wild, this exciting skill saves poicephalus parrots from being eaten by predators. In the home, however, the question of whether a pet bird should be allowed to fly is constantly debated by aviculturists.

Dangers lurk everywhere, not just in the African savannah. Perhaps you have other pets, or maybe you enjoy the feeling of fresh air that comes from open doors and windows. Sometimes peril waits in the most innocent places—a sink half full of dishwater or a stove burner accidentally left turned on. All of these common situations can prove deadly for a parrot allowed to fly freely around his home.

If you choose to keep your Senegal fully flighted, you must take certain precautions to ensure his safety. This means completely parrot-proofing your home and making sure that all household members and visitors understand the importance of following the related house rules. Exterior doors and windows must be kept closed at all times when your bird is outside his cage, and everyone must always check his location before closing an interior door to prevent it from closing on one of his wings or feet. Many a wing has been broken this way, but the results can be even worse.

For some owners, one of the most practical ways to keep their parrots safe is by clipping their wings. This common procedure of trimming a bird's primary flight feathers to limit his mobility does not hurt the bird and is often likened to a nail trim

A Clean Bill of Health

Because birds are covered with feathers, it can be nearly impossible to notice a cut or scratch on your Senegal's skin. Perhaps even more worrisome is how difficult it can be to discover a suspicious lump on your parrot if you do not handle him regularly. Also, because birds are so adept at hiding signs of illness (a skill that protects them from predators in the wild), it is imperative that we routinely look for symptoms of illness or injury in our pet parrots. This certainly includes behavioral signs of an affliction, but it should always begin with a simple physical inspection. This can easily be accomplished during the grooming process.

When you have your bird wrapped in a towel for his nail clipping, use the opportunity to gently check his entire body for any abnormalities. While your Senegal is basking in the warm water of your shower, inspect his skin. You'll be amazed by how much of the skin is visible between his soaked feathers.

Don't overlook those feathers themselves, though. Dull, rough, or dirty feathers (a sign that your bird isn't preening) are all possible symptoms of illness. Also, look for discoloration, misshapen feathers, and bald areas that may indicate feather picking—a common response to poor health.

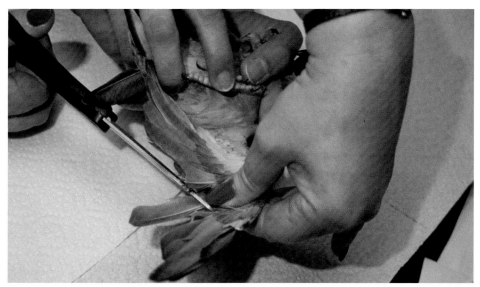

If you decide to clip your Senegal's wings, have a veterinarian or professional bird groomer show you how first.

or haircut. It also does not totally prevent a parrot from flying; it merely makes it more difficult for him to lift himself with his wings. A clipped bird can usually lower himself for a safe landing if he decides to fly off the top of his cage, for instance. He just won't be able to go higher and higher or maintain ongoing flight. Even a clipped bird can dart around impressively, though, so it is still wise to bird-proof your home even if you elect to trim your Senegal's wings.

Opponents of wing clipping emphasize that flying is excellent exercise. A bird who is allowed to fly regularly will develop improved muscle tone and better cardiac health. He may also be a happier pet. If you own other animals, free flying may allow your

bird to encounter them more easily, but it can also help him escape them if necessary.

If you favor clipping, make sure that the procedure is done by an experienced individual each time it is needed (typically after a molt). I strongly recommend that new owners never attempt this task themselves. Even small mistakes can lead to feather picking, phobias, and serious injuries or death. The effects aren't always immediate. Some resulting problems can take weeks or even months to develop after an improper clip.

I consider clipping to be a personal choice, one that must often be made based on the needs of an individual parrot. Some aviculturists insist that clipping can help hinder aggression.

Grooming: A Two-Way Street?

When my Senegal parrot MacLeod sits on my husband's shoulder, one of Mac's favorite pastimes is preening his human daddy. This is made even more thrilling for Mac if my husband hasn't yet shaved because the only thing Mac enjoys more than going over each and every strand of hair on my husband's head is gently running his little gray tongue over as many whiskers on my husband's face as he can manage before his daddy can no longer stand the tickling.

Mac also gets preened in this process. My husband will invariably rub Mac's head in search of pinfeathers, developing feathers that can cause a parrot discomfort until their waxy tops are gradually removed through preening. This rubbing prompts Mac to lower his little head and lean into my husband's neck. Birds preen (or clean) themselves at an impressive

Jardine's parrots and other poicephalus enjoy preening their favorite people.

rate, running nearly every feather on their bodies through their beaks several times each day. As they preen themselves, they cover their feathers with oil from their uropygial gland to help make them waterproof. Parrots cannot, however, reach the feathers on their own heads. Mac and my Senegal-Meyer's parrot Jake spend time regularly preening each other whenever they are out of their cages, and it is obvious that this activity is just as emotional as physical. Sure, it is a practical pursuit, but preening time is also bonding time.

Of course, there are countless other activities ripe with bonding potential for you and your Senegal. Few are as hands-on, so to speak, as preening. It's a great way to show your parrot that you love him, and even if you're on the ticklish side, it's nice to know that he cares about helping with your "pinfeathers" too.

Others argue that some parrots thrive only when allowed full flight. I keep two of my parrots fully flighted and one clipped. This works best for my birds; you must do what works best for yours.

Molting

Like dogs, who shed dead hair from their bodies seasonally, birds also go through a form of shedding called molting. When parrots molt, their feathers fall out when new ones begin growing in their place. Molting may occur as a result of various external and internal forces, including the changing amount of daylight and temperature fluctuations, a particular bird's diet, and sex and species. Interestingly, different feathers from various parts of a parrot's body will molt at different rates. It may take a young Senegal an entire year or more to complete his first molt, with his tail feathers in particular taking the longest to fall out and replenish themselves fully.

Senegals need an especially nutritious diet during molting.

Outside their natural environment and inside our homes, Senegals will usually molt more dramatically due to the wide spectrum of temperatures to which we expose them. Conventional use of air conditioning in the summer and heat in the winter can hurl pet birds into a nearly constant cycle of molting. Although the molting process itself is entirely normal, this faster-paced rhythm will often increase a parrot's metabolism and stress level, making a sensible diet an even more important factor in his health. Certain amino acids are necessary for proper feather growth and development, so it is especially important that your Senegal eat a diet rich in these and other nutrients during a molt. This can help prevent feather picking, an undesirable activity that can sometimes be triggered by excessive molting and the stress that accompanies it.

5

A Healthy Life

Birds are adept at hiding signs of illness until a problem has become serious. In the wild, this instinctual ability protects a parrot from being ostracized by his flock members, or worse, becoming an easy meal for predators. A pet Senegal, on the other hand, can suffer dire consequences if his owner isn't equally proficient at recognizing illness before it becomes a bigger threat to his health. This makes routine veterinary care a top priority.

Finding an Avian Veterinarian

At one time, finding an avian veterinarian was a daunting task. It typically involved scouring the phone book in search of a vet who treated exotic pets and frequently required a bit of travel, especially if the owner lived in the country or suburbs. Fortunately, avian veterinarians are now more plentiful, even in smaller towns and cities.

Finding your ideal vet may prove a bit more challenging, but it shouldn't be difficult, provided you follow a few simple guidelines. First and foremost, feel free to utilize technology, but never rely on it as your only research tool. The Internet can instantly lead you to multiple avian veterinarians in your area. Certainly, you may find browsing a particular doctor's website

helpful; however, nothing replaces the value of good old-fashioned word of mouth. I recommend leaving the search engines for follow-up research once you have received one or more recommendations from more reliable sources. These may include your local

All parrots are experts at hiding illness until they are very sick, so you must become skilled at recognizing the signs of sickness early.

caged bird society, a humane society or other rescue organization, your Senegal's breeder, or a nearby pet supply store.

Once you have an initial list of names, this is the time to visit each doctor's website for more information about her practice. Find out as much as you can before calling to schedule an initial appointment and asking for a tour of the facilities. You may even find a virtual tour online, but remember that nothing compares to meeting the staff personally.

If a veterinary hospital doesn't have a website, this by no means indicates that it is an inferior choice. What matters most is that you feel comfortable with the staff. Large hospitals filled with state-of-the-art equipment may be a benefit, but it also usually means that the costs of services will be higher. What you want is a good fit for you and your Senegal, not necessarily a fancy waiting room filled with pretty furniture.

If you get a bad feeling about a specific person or practice, keep looking. The number of US households owning birds is rapidly approaching 6.5 million. This sizable group of pet owners has created an important niche in the veterinary community for doctors trained to treat our winged patients, and more and more capable vets are serving this important purpose.

The Vet Visit

Even if your breeder assures you that your Senegal has recently been

Proper Toweling Procedure

If you must restrain your Senegal, use a towel. Your hand should rest on the outside of the shroud with your thumb near the opening of your bird's ear and your index finger above his head, holding it gently but securely. The towel should wrap around the bird's body and fall just below his mouth—this will provide him with a safe chewing material. A parrot will usually transfer his anxiety about being restrained onto the towel instead of the person holding him. Avoid using gloves, as they can leave your bird with an unpleasant connotation to human hands.

checked by a veterinarian, it is wise to have your own vet examine your bird shortly after bringing him home. Small problems can occasionally be overlooked, and the best way to prevent any issue from turning into a larger one is early diagnosis. Furthermore, if you bought your bird from a pet store offering a health guarantee, the contract may require that he see a vet within a certain number of days or hours following the purchase. Once your parrot's good health has been confirmed, he should only need routine exams annually or if any health concerns arise between these visits.

Plan your Senegal's yearly checkup for a mild time of the year in terms of weather. Transporting him during either extremely hot or cold temperatures can be dangerous. If you must take your bird outside in the middle of winter, warm up your vehicle and cover his carrier appropriately. Likewise, provide your parrot with plenty of water during a summer trip to the vet and shield him from the sun, even while riding inside an air-conditioned automobile.

Before beginning the physical exam, your veterinarian will ask you a number of questions pertaining to your Senegal's history. Your bird's age will be recorded on his chart, along with various other information, such as sex (if known), where you got him, what you are feeding him, and any identified health or behavior problems. This is an excellent time to address any concerns you may have about any of these issues. Never be afraid to ask your vet questions, and always answer questions your vet asks you as thoroughly as you can. This will help provide your Senegal with the best care possible.

Senegals will stretch their wings periodically; holding a wing in an odd position or letting it droop can indicate an illness or injury.

Your veterinarian will then observe your parrot as he sits on a perch designed for weighing birds. Some vets prefer to use a bowl-style scale with or without a cover. My Senegal's vet jokingly refers to the weigh-in portion of the checkup as "birdie in the pot" because he uses a cover on his metal bowl-style scale.

For the vet to fully examine your Senegal, he must be held securely in a towel or small blanket. This will enable her to feel the keel bone (more commonly called the breastbone) and check for any abnormalities there or elsewhere on your bird's body.

A thorough doctor will ask to inspect the droppings left in your Senegal's carrier, as this is an effective means of identifying underlying illness. This is not the only way to check for sickness, though. A culture or gram stain can also be performed to rule out viruses and infections. This is done by swabbing the inside of your bird's mouth and the vent (the area just under his tail).

Blood tests, though available, are not typically a part of a routine avian exam unless suggested for a particular reason or requested by an owner. When performed, these can help identify any vitamin or mineral deficiencies, as well as a common avian disease, psittacosis. You may certainly use a blood test to conclusively determine your Senegal's sex, but this is generally a pricier way of doing so than testing feathers. Vaccines are used primarily in younger birds specifically to prevent psittacine beak and feather disease (PBFD) and polyomavirus, so your bird most likely won't need any shots during his visit.

Finally, your vet will perform any necessary grooming that you prefer not to do yourself. This may include nail trimming, wing clipping, and beak grinding. She may also instruct you on how to handle these tasks at home if you are interested in learning.

General Signs That Your Bird Might Be Sick

As you get to know your bird, you will learn about his typical habits and behaviors—what is normal for him. You'll be surprised by how quickly you will notice when something isn't right. Sometimes this will be tangible, like an area of matted feathers on your bird's head or neck or a growth on his skin. Other times the difference may be more subtle, like a slight change in his vocalizations or mood. Even if you find it difficult to articulate the problem, it is important to bring it to your veterinarian's attention. In some cases, acting quickly just might save your bird's life.

Common indications that your bird might be ill include weight loss, a decreased appetite, and general lethargy. Also, look for changes in the appearance of your bird's feathers; dull or missing feathers not associated with molting are cause for concern. More pronounced symptoms of illness include trouble breathing, bleeding, and difficulty balancing.

This Shouldn't Hurt a Bit

Bringing your child along to your Senegal's annual veterinary checkup can be very educational, but a few precautions should be taken to make sure that the youngster isn't alarmed by any of the tasks your vet performs. Let her know that the veterinarian will need to examine your parrot thoroughly. Describe how the vet will secure the bird in a small blanket or towel while she spreads each wing and checks for any abnormalities in his skin, feathers, or general appearance. Explain that if wing clipping, nail trimming, or beak grinding is necessary, this will also be done at this time. Although a parrot may become more tolerant of these procedures as time goes on, there is usually at least some resistance on his behalf. He may even screech in a way that makes your child worry that he is in pain.

Assure your child that your Senegal is in capable hands and that his good health is much more important than a minor amount of discomfort. To minimize the anxiety your parrot feels (and to make the exam as quick as possible for him), it is vital that your child be on her best behavior. Parrots are incredibly perceptive creatures. If your child is upset by the exam, or worse, if she has a temper tantrum during the visit, this can increase your bird's stress dramatically. For this reason, it may be helpful to bring along another adult to escort your child from the room if necessary while the vet finishes the checkup.

Seek veterinary treatment immediately if your bird develops any of these problems, as they are signs of a medical emergency.

Avian Illnesses

Aspergillosis

Aspergillosis is a fungal infection that affects a parrot's respiratory and digestive systems. Symptoms include a clicking sound during breathing; gasping; and wheezing. The infection develops when a bird inhales mold spores within his environment. Just because a bird is exposed to these spores, though, does not mean that he will succumb to the illness. Birds under stress are far more vulnerable to becoming sick. These include parrots suffering from malnutrition or other problems affecting the immune system, birds in breeding programs, and those who are shipped from one locationto another.

A blood test can reveal an elevated white blood cell count and mild anemia (both indicators of the infection), but conclusive diagnosis is often difficult. Aspergillosis can sometimes be successfully treated with immunostimulants, but surgery may also be necessary. As with so many avian illnesses, the best plan of attack is prevention.

All types of fungi grow quickly in dark and dank environments, so keep your bird's cage as clean and dry as possible. Changing cage linings daily will help keep fecal matter and moldy bits of uneaten food away from your Senegal. Remove dishes filled with highly perishable foods after an hour or two of being offered to prevent spoilage. Also, always present your bird's food in clean dishes and use clean knives and other utensils when preparing his fresh fruits and veggies. Just a little extra time each day will help keep that mold away.

Chlamydiosis (Psittacosis)

Chlamydiosis is a bacterial illness passed through contact with an infected bird's droppings and other secretions. Commonly called psittacosis or parrot fever, this disease causes respiratory distress. Other symptoms include decreased appetite, diarrhea, lethargy, nasal discharge, sneezing, weight loss, and green or yellow-green urine. This last sign may seem a bit confusing because normal Senegal droppings are often green in color. The feces part of your bird's dropping should in fact be either green or brown, but the urine part should be clear and watery, not green. Another section of the dropping, known as urates, should be an opaque white-beige and is not an indication of illness.

If your bird contracts psittacosis, treatment with a broad-spectrum antibiotic will be necessary. Dosing is often required for as long as 45 days to fully eradicate the infection. In left untreated, the disease can be fatal.

What differentiates this avian illness from most others is that it is considered a zoonotic disease, meaning that it can be transmitted from animals to

Signs That Your Senegal Needs Emergency Care

Seek veterinary care immediately if your bird experiences any of the following symptoms:

- bleeding
- bite wounds
- burns (remember, hot food can burn your Senegal's crop!)
- difficulty breathing
- discharge from the eyes or nostrils
- equilibrium problems (balancing on a perch, etc.)
- limping
- lumps or masses
- seizures
- sneezing (but know that some parrots learn to mimic their humans' sneezes)
- sudden, unexplained weight loss
- undigested food or blood in droppings
- vomiting (not to be confused with affection regurgitation)

humans. Fortunately, most zoonotic diseases are not passed from pet parrots but rather from poultry and other wild birds. People who work regularly with parrots, such as breeders and pet store employees, are at an elevated risk, though, and should always use caution when cleaning cages and coming in contact with fecal matter. When chlamydiosis is spread to humans, it is called ornithosis and presents with symptoms such as fever and chills, soreness in the muscles and joints, and chest pain. Ornithosis can also be treated with antibiotics, usually for 21 days or more. If left untreated, pneumonia can develop, so prompt and thorough treatment is essential.

Polyomavirus (PVD)

First discovered in 1981 in budgies, polyoma is a highly contagious virus that typically affects very young birds. Symptoms include appetite loss, dehydration, diarrhea, lethargy, feather abnormalities, rapid and ongoing weight loss (but with a swollen abdomen), tremors, vomiting,

Your Senegal will fluff up his feathers on occasion, but if he stays fluffed up, he may be ill.

and hemorrhaging at the site of an injection.

Although polyoma does not affect human beings, the virus almost always proves fatal to young birds (typically those between two weeks and five months of age). It often kills adult parrots who have not been vaccinated against the virus as well. However, even parrots who show no symptoms can become carriers of this deadly illness that targets virtually every system in the avian body. For this important reason, all young Senegals should be vaccinated

against polyoma before being sold. Polyoma can be prevented, but there is currently no cure.

Psittacine Beak and Feather Disease (PBFD)

The signs of PBFD include abnormal feather growth (short, clubbed or curled feathers, for instance), feather loss, and fractures in the bird's beak. Although these problems may at first appear merely cosmetic, PBFD is a serious medical condition. The disease is caused by a virus that literally kills the cells of an infected bird's beak and feathers. It also destroys the bird's immune system, leaving him susceptible to countless other bacterial infections simultaneously.

Parrots can be tested for PBFD, but there is currently no known treatment. Some birds have been known to spontaneously recover, but this is rare and virtually unheard of in severe situations. Chronic cases cause a parrot to experience difficulty eating, which leads to significant weight loss, and consequently, death. Because the disease is communicable, it is recommended that young birds be vaccinated as early as 14 days of age. Vaccination is not, however, recommended for parrots already stricken with the disease, as it can actually intensify the illness in these birds.

Senegal Weight and Health

Keeping your Senegal fit and trim is one of the most basic parts of proper

Nonstick Coatings Are Everywhere

If you own nonstick cookware, one of the most important steps in bird-proofing your home is to replace these pots and pans with a safer cooking surface, such as uncoated stainless steel. Nonstick surfaces emit noxious fumes that can kill birds, but it is important to note that cookware is not the only nonstick danger. Clothes dryers, curling irons, and numerous other household appliances are made with this popular coating. It may not be feasible to remove nonstick coatings from our homes entirely, but we can take sensible precautions. Do not situate your bird's cage in your kitchen because even countertop bread machines and conventional ovens frequently contain nonstick surfaces. If you have a laundry room, set your ironing board up there and never near your bird, as both ironing board covers and the irons themselves are also typically made with this material. If you allow your Senegal to shower with you, return him to his cage before you blow-dry your hair, and never use your hairdryer on your bird because it too likely harbors a nonstick coating.

avian health care. Overweight birds are at greater risk of countless afflictions, including heart disease, liver disease, tumors, and respiratory distress.

Preventing obesity means helping to prevent illness.

How can you tell if your Senegal is overweight? For starters, you should weigh your bird regularly. This will help establish a normal range for his weight and alert you to an increase before it becomes a more substantial one. Additionally, watch your bird. A parrot carrying too much weight will

Avian First Aid

Treating an extremely ill or injured parrot is a job for a veterinarian trained to care for avian species. For this important reason, the purpose of your Senegal's first-aid kit is to help you stabilize your pet while you seek professional treatment in the event that he needs emergency care. If your bird has experienced an injury, call your vet's office immediately to warn the staff of your imminent arrival. This will help the veterinary staff prepare and save time that may be crucial in your pet's care. As difficult as it may be, the best thing you can do for your bird is to remain calm—and remember to grab the kit you have assembled with the following items:

- aloe vera gel (for cooling burns or scrapes)
- antiseptic towelettes (for cleaning wounds or hands)
- gauze and scissors (for wrapping a more serious cut)
- gram scale (for weighing your bird regularly; extreme fluctuations are an indicator of illness)
- index card with emergency phone numbers, including your veterinarian and poison control
- notepad and pen (for taking down any instructions from your vet)
- oral syringe or eye dropper (for administering medications as directed by your veterinarian)
- plastic bandages (for your own use in case your parrot bites, a common reaction in injured birds)
- saline solution (for irrigating wounds)
- secure carrier (affixed with a full water bottle if you will have a long drive to your vet's office)
- styptic powder (for speeding clotting in the event of bleeding)
- towel (for catching your bird in a precarious situation or covering his carrier during transport to the vet in cold weather)
- tweezers (for removing feathers, splinters, or ticks as directed by your veterinarian)

usually have a wider than normal stance. He may also have a small roll of fat under his beak, similar to a human's so-called double chin. If your Senegal is too heavy, you may even notice that his feather tracts have separated due to fat under his skin, causing bald patches in certain places on his body.

If your Senegal has become overweight, talk to your veterinarian about adjusting his diet and exercise routine. It won't happen overnight, but with the advice of a professional, you can return your bird to a healthy weight. It will almost certainly improve his health and lengthen his life.

If you get your Senegal used to feeding from a syringe on occasion, it will be easier to medicate him should the need arise.

Senior Bird Care

When fed a healthy diet and brought in for routine veterinary care, your Senegal parrot has the potential to live for several decades. As he gets older, though, his needs will change a bit. Fortunately, most of the challenges presented by your parrot's senior years can be met fairly easily. Moreover, there are many ways that you can help make your bird's life an even longer and more enjoyable one.

Feeding nutritious foods is important throughout your Senegal's life, but it is especially important that this healthy habit continue as he gets older. Feeding fresh fruits and vegetables and limiting seeds and sugary foods will help keep your bird fit and trim. Obese birds face greater health risks as they age, so stack the odds in your parrot's favor by keeping the fat and calories to a minimum. Like people, parrots experience a decreased metabolism with age, leaving them more vulnerable to weight gain. Senior birds also need slightly less protein. Instead, offer foods such as such as papaya and pineapple regularly. These fruits contain enzymes called proteases that activate certain immune system cells.

Encouraging your bird to remain active is also an essential step to keeping him feeling like a spring chicken. As parrots age, they lose

Stress Management

Even for a parrot, stress is a necessary part of life. In healthy doses it can increase a bird's energy level and alertness. When excessive, though, stress can leave your bird more vulnerable to illness and injury. Below is a list of circumstances that can increase your Senegal's stress level. If any of these situations applies to your bird, keep a closer eye on his health so that any problems that may arise can be addressed quickly and efficiently. Some events are unavoidable, but limiting them will help keep your parrot's stress in the healthy range. For example, if you buy your bird a new cage, try to avoid the other items on the list until he has adapted to his new surroundings.

- absence of a familiar person or fellow pet (due to a divorce or death, for instance)
- change in cage placement in home
- changes in routine (such as feeding time, owner's work schedule, etc.)
- dirty cage
- lack of exercise
- lack of sleep
- new cage (even if it is bigger and better than the one he is accustomed to)
- new caregiver (such as a pet sitter)
- new home (either moving or joining the household of a new owner)
- new person or pet within the home
- poor nutrition
- travel
- other sudden changes

Breeders should vaccinate their Senegals for PVD and PBFD before selling them.

skin elasticity and experience muscle deterioration, stiff joints, and poor feather condition. One of the best ways to combat these problems is regular exercise. Even older birds enjoy flying or wing flapping, and all birds need time outside their cages each day.

Finally, talk to your veterinarian about increasing the frequency of your older Senegal's routine checkups from once to twice a year. The timing of this proactive step can vary, depending on your individual parrot's overall health and lifestyle, but the rewards can be invaluable. The best defense against many afflictions is prompt diagnosis.

Early diagnosis is especially important if your older bird develops a malignant tumor because avian cancer rates increase dramatically with age. Although not always cancerous, tumors may appear on a parrot's skin or on his internal organs. The primary symptom of an internal tumor is lameness, but this may not occur until the growth has progressed to an extremely dangerous point or metastasized (spread) to other internal organs. Your veterinarian may be able to detect an internal tumor during your bird's semi-annual examination while treatment is still possible, but you must provide the opportunity for this lifesaving discovery by making that extra appointment.

6

The Well-Behaved Senegal

"Good boy!" My Senegal parrot MacLeod enthusiastically says this at least once every day. He has heard my husband and I say it to him so often that he regularly praises his own actions, as well as those of our other parrots, our dogs, and even our ten-year-old son. Mac enjoys "being good" himself and rewarding others with his abundant praise whenever he sees fit.

As evidenced by MacLeod and countless other birds, parrots truly enjoy learning, and the things owners can teach them are never ending. How we teach them, however, is just as important as what we teach them.

Basic Training

In addition to being fun for both you and your Senegal, training is a necessary part of parrot ownership. Most people who want to become parrot owners wish to handle their birds. If this will be possible, your first goal must be forging a positive relationship with your Senegal. This can be accomplished in many ways all at once: through trust and patience and by using effective means of communication. Training is basically just that–communication, finding a way to express your wishes to your bird and watching him for signs that he understands what you are telling him.

Eventually, your Senegal may begin to use language to express himself to you. Although this can be an exciting part of owning a parrot, it is not a necessary step to good communication with your bird. Some of the most meaningful exchanges you will ever have with your bird may involve no words at all. I am always annoyed when someone refers to my parrots as somehow less important than other kinds of pets. The relationship between a parrot and his owner can be just as special as one between a dog and his owner.

With consistent, patient training, Senegals are capable of learning many fun tricks.

Positive Reinforcement

The only way to teach a parrot anything is with positive reinforcement. Punishing a bird is just as ineffective as using negative reinforcement with a dog, cat, or human being. The only thing that is taught through punishment is fear. And the best way to ruin your relationship with any bird is to give him reason to fear you. Parrots have long memories, and they hold grudges.

I recommend using praise whenever your bird does something good and whenever possible, ignoring him when he does something undesirable. This can be challenging if you are trying to teach him not to bite, but even then, ignoring the bad behavior really is the best approach if you can manage it. If you cannot, create a safe spot for a birdie time-out. The spot can be anywhere at all except your parrot's cage—you never want him to associate his cage with bad behavior. If your Senegal is biting as a means of getting back to his cage, placing him on a T-stand in another area of your home will show him that biting won't get him what he wants.

I also encourage owners to use edible rewards to treat their birds for good behavior. You must be careful, though, not to overuse them. A poicephalus parrot is just as prone to becoming overweight as any other animal that is overfed. Also, using food as a reward each and every time your bird does what you want may make compliance dependent on the edible treat. Instead, use food intermittently, a proven strategy in successful training.

Socialization

In addition to training your bird, you should place socializing him high on your list of priorities. Many birds are remarkably well behaved for their beloved owners but turn into entirely different animals when in the presence of another pet or a new person. Although your Senegal will generally only encounter other people when they visit your home, there are a few people he must encounter on a regular basis outside these walls—particularly if you bring him to a professional for grooming.

If you enjoy the fact that your Senegal seems to prefer you to anyone else, you are not alone. Many parrot owners delight in the intense bond shared with their birds. You must consider what will happen to your bird, though, in the event that you need to

Rewards in a Nutshell

Edible rewards are excellent motivators in training, but it is important to keep them small. If a treat takes too much time to eat, it can distract from the training process. Soft-shelled nuts work well, as do seeds. Because seeds should be limited in your bird's diet, they will be especially appealing to him—a genuine treat. Working with your bird before feeding time is fine, but never withhold food as a means of making edible treats more effective.

spend time in the hospital or if you wish to take a vacation someday. It is also wise to choose a guardian for your bird in the event of your death. Because parrots live such long lives, it is important that you have a plan in place for your bird, just as you would for a child.

The best way to socialize your Senegal is to invite as many responsible friends and family members as possible to interact with him. The more comfortable your bird is with dealing with these people, the more likely he will be to tolerate other people. Be discriminating in your selection of the people you encourage to handle your bird, though. People who are fearful of birds or animals in general are usually bad candidates, as are people who tend not to follow simple guidelines.

Children may be completely appropriate choices but only if they are old enough to understand your instructions and responsible enough to heed them.

Talking

One of the most exciting aspects of owning a parrot is that your pet may actually be able to talk to you someday. Although experts debate the intellectual depth of parrot speech, a bird's spoken words undeniably surpass the capabilities of nearly all other animals in terms of verbal communication. Senegals are hardly the most proficient talkers in the world of parrots, but they can learn an impressive number of words and phrases with surprising clarity. It is imperative, though, that you do

Use small rewards during training to prevent them from becoming a lengthy distraction.

not purchase or adopt any bird with predetermined expectations of speech–some parrots, even African greys, will never talk.

Oftentimes a Senegal will begin speaking before he has even completely settled into his owner's home. My Senegal's first words were spoken while I was teaching him the step-up command. He had heard me repeat the instruction so many times that eventually he began saying the words as he performed the action. His other early phrases were also things he heard me say frequently, such as his name. To date I haven't actually taught him a single word or phrase. Everything he says (approximately 50 words or phrases and numerous sounds and whistles) he learned on his own, just from listening to my husband, my son, and me speaking normally around our home.

Although I doubt that Mac fully understands everything he says, I have witnessed countless of his responses to external stimuli that can only be described as meaningfully appropriate, many of which required a certain amount of thought on his behalf. Mac began calling me *Mac's Mommy* several years ago, assumingly from hearing my husband say this in his presence. More recently he started asking me a question: "Are you Mac's Mommy?" Whenever he repeats this, I answer in the affirmative with a

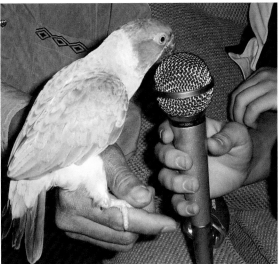

Recording your Senegal when he talks is not only fun, but it can also help you identify him if he is lost or stolen.

smile. My smile is partly because I find the phrase so endearing and partly because I am so impressed that Mac somehow strung these words together without ever having heard someone else say them as a question. After one such instance, Mac decided to tweak his sentence a bit. "Are you Jake's Mommy?" he inquired. He seems pleased when I tell him that I am, but like his understanding of the phrase itself, I have no way of proving this conclusively.

One might argue that one of the reasons Mac is such a talented talker is that he is male. In many avian species, the males are on average more likely to speak than females. Bear in mind, however, that this is just a generalization. Many female Senegals

Student Teachers

and other poicephalus parrots can learn a broad variety of words and phrases.

If you are trying to teach your Senegal to talk, work with him in the morning and early evening. These are the times when parrots are most inclined to vocalize and learn. Keep the training sessions short, no longer than 20 minutes. You should also focus on just a single word or phrase at a time. Avoid words containing the letters *l* and *r* in the beginning, as these are difficult sounds for parrots to enunciate.

Food can be an excellent motivator, so begin each training session by offering your bird a small treat, and then offer another when he begins to mimic what you are saying. Reward him even if the words aren't spoken exactly. In the beginning, you want to reward the effort; with a particularly quiet bird, this may mean that you offer him a peanut just for mumbling a bit.

Some owners swear by using CDs or leaving the television or radio on to encourage talking. While this may be helpful when used in addition to more interactive training, I think that a bird is most impressionable to learning words or phrases he hears other household members saying on a regular basis. Repetition is crucial, but so is tone of voice, mood, and the laughter or other reactions that usually follow words spoken between people.

Whistling is another common ability among birds. Jacob (my Senegal-Meyer's parrot) in particular is so adept at this task and mimicking other noises that I have nicknamed him my little sound machine. Some avian experts advise owners against encouraging whistling before a bird begins using words. They insist that once a bird begins to whistle, he will prefer this behavior to talking. I can't say for certain whether this is true for all poicephalus parrots, but I do know that Jake's vocabulary is about half the size of Mac's. Jake is much more likely to imitate the ring of the telephone or the beep of the microwave than to use sentences like Mac does. Jake primarily uses monosyllabic words, but more often we hear him laughing, sneezing, and coughing when we do these things. He taught himself the latter two sounds one winter while I was fighting a nasty cold.

In many ways, owning a parrot is similar to having a small child in the home. You must be patient, kind, and constantly vigilant of your words. If you do accidentally say something unsavory, don't gasp or giggle. Senegals have a special knack for being able to tell when you don't want something repeated and saying it anyway.

The Basics of Handling Your Senegal

To teach your parrot the step-up command, begin by placing a steady index finger in front of him and gently pushing against his belly. This effectively forces him to move from his perch to your hand. As soon as he begins this move, say the words *step up.* Even when your Senegal starts stepping toward your hand as it nears him, continue repeating the phrase to ensure that he learns what the words mean. Many birds will start saying the phrase along with their owners and even use it as a method of asking for attention.

Repetition is vital when teaching this command. Move your Senegal from one hand to the other or from person to person repeatedly, which also helps with socialization. Eventually, your parrot will consistently step up as soon as he sees you move your hand in front of him without any verbal prompting whatsoever.

Some owners prefer to use a perch or a natural branch for teaching a parrot the step-up command. Called stick training, this technique can help you avoid bites from an uneasy bird, but it must be done even more gently than with the hand or you might trigger an aggressive response. Stick training can be extremely helpful if your Senegal flies off to a high or difficult to

I Heard It Through the Grapevine

No matter how hard you try to train your bird to say certain things or perform different commands, he will undoubtedly learn at least a few things entirely on his own. These may be words or behaviors that he learns just from observing his environment. MacLeod has bestowed Jacob with a nickname all his own, McJake. My husband and I joke that apparently Mac thinks that all poicephalus descend from a clan of Scottish parrots. And both Mac and Jake meow, even though we have never owned a cat in the time we've had our birds. When Scot and I were first married, however, we rented an apartment with very thin walls and neighbors who owned two indoor cats.

reach place. It can also make it possible for a younger child to safely handle your bird, always with the supervision of an adult, of course.

Be sure to hold the end of the perch supporting your parrot raised higher than the end with your hand. This will discourage him from climbing onto your arm. Also, don't keep your arm parallel to the floor, as this too may invite your bird to move from the perch onto you.

Potty Training

Many people do not realize that parrots can be potty trained. My pionus parrot, Raffi, effectively trained herself, promptly flying from my shoulder to her cage whenever she needed to relieve herself. Once I realized what she was doing, I began praising her efforts, but she truly did the work herself. Other parrots are less concerned about defecating in the proper spot. I doubt that Jacob will ever be potty trained, which is why I make an effort to return him to his cage every 15 minutes or so to avoid having to clean his droppings from my clothes or carpeting.

Potty-trained birds who wish to remain with their owners may sometimes hold their droppings for extended periods, much the way a young child might do when she is doing something enjoyable and doesn't wish to take a bathroom break. This can be extremely dangerous for birds because it puts them at a greater risk for bacterial infections.

The best way to potty train your Senegal to eliminate in a specific area is to praise him whenever he does it naturally. Never scold him for going in the wrong spot, though. He may confuse your admonishment as a

One of the first things you should teach your Senegal is to step onto your finger consistently.

response to the act of his relieving himself. Also, don't react to the mess if your bird defecates on you, as this can spark a fun pastime. Whenever your bird is away from his cage for more than 10 to 15 minutes, return him to the top of the structure. (You need not put him inside.) Wait for him to eliminate and then praise him for a job well done. Eventually, he should be able to go on command when you time it right. If you are lucky, your bird may even remember to make the pit stop on his own like Raffi does.

Problem Behaviors

The director of a large-scale rescue organization once told me that the biggest problem affecting bird behavior is actually the bird owners themselves. She explained that as human beings, we often do not understand the inherent nature of our parrots and their specialized needs. I try to remember this conversation whenever I approach a problem behavior with my parrots. I first try to decide what role I might be playing in the problem; I then try to find a solution that will help change whatever I am doing wrong—and in turn correct the problem.

Biting

The two keys to dealing with biting are first, preventing it whenever possible, and second, responding in the proper way. To prevent biting, though, we must begin by understanding why birds bite in the first place. I assure you that this is not a random act. Birds always bite for a

reason; identifying that reason will help you change your own behavior in order to change your bird's response.

The main reason most birds bite is to communicate that they are displeased with what you are doing. For instance, the first thing you may do when you wish to offer your bird attention is retrieve him from his cage. Imagine if someone were to reach inside your home when she decided that it was time spend time with you and literally pulled you away from whatever you were doing. You would likely be pretty upset, right? This is no different for your Senegal. A bird who feels ripped from the safety and security of his cage will react with his most basic instinct of biting to let you know that he is unhappy. To prevent this reaction, the next time you want to offer your bird some time outside his cage, do just that: Offer it. Open his cage door and wait for him to decide that he wants to come out on his own. This one strategy could eliminate your bird's biting problem altogether. Birds in general tend to feel extremely territorial about their cages and will go to extremes to protect this special space from intruders.

Another common reason parrots bite is that they have been trained, albeit inadvertently, to do so. What do you do when your bird bites you? If you return him to his cage, you are probably teaching him that when he bites, he gets what he wants. Think of this in terms of a child who throws a temper tantrum because she wants

Respecting Your Bird's Space

Although most birds are somewhat territorial when it comes to their cages, extreme reactions can become a problem for both you and your pet. Certainly, you will need to enter your bird's cage for routine tasks, such as feeding and cleaning. If your bird tries to bite you at these times, it can make these everyday chores extremely taxing. There is a difference, however, between respectfully entering your Senegal's cage when you need to and barging in whenever you feel like it. Remember, your bird's cage is the only space he has that belongs to him alone. When you come home or enter the room, you may be anxious to visit with your parrot, and he may look forward to this time with you as well. Allow him time to transition, though. By just opening the door and speaking to him, you invite him to share some meaningful time with you. If you open the door and snatch him from his perch, however, this special time instead becomes a mandatory evacuation. Once your bird steps outside the bars, you may then approach him and ask him to step up. He should comply, but if he quickly flies back to his cage, respect his wishes and give him some time before pursuing him further. Even if he goes back inside his cage, you may still leave the door, and the invitation, open. For the sake of his safety, though, don't forget to close it before leaving the room.

a candy bar. If she falls to the floor kicking and screaming and you react by giving her the candy, you will almost certainly see more kicking and screaming in the future. Your Senegal is in many ways like a human two-year-old but one who will never grow up, so while your child will eventually move beyond this terrible stage, your bird will continue to bite to win a trip back to his cage.

You may not think that your bird's biting is a true problem if he is nipping your clothing instead of your skin or if he isn't hurting you when he bites. While this is certainly a less severe form of the problem, biting should never be encouraged. Many owners will try to distract a parrot from

gnawing on their clothes by providing him with a small treat to occupy his busy beak. Don't do this! This too teaches a bird to bite by rewarding the behavior. Distracting your bird is an excellent way of addressing the issue, but avoid using food for this at all costs. Instead, use sounds and movements to sway your Senegal's attention away from this habit.

As difficult as it may sound, the best reaction to biting is none at all. Parrots love to elicit strong reactions of any kind from their owners. Hearing you shriek (in either pain or delight) is great fun for them. This doesn't mean that you should allow your bird to repeatedly attack you, but try to wait to put him down (preferably on a T-stand or other safe place away from his cage) until after the biting has stopped. You can shorten this time by subtly moving your arm, causing your bird to pay more attention to his balance than his plan of attack.

If your bird's biting is an ongoing problem, you may need to seek the assistance of a professional behaviorist. Your breeder or veterinarian should be able to refer you to someone in your area who specializes in helping parrot owners deal with this kind of habitual problem.

Aviculturists tend to split down the middle on the issue of allowing a bird to perch on his human's shoulder. Many vets and other professionals discourage this habit, as it leaves the owner extremely vulnerable to injury if a parrot bites. Owners must be aware that this is a very real threat. The beak of a Senegal is strong enough to do significant damage to the human face. Even the best-behaved birds can be unpredictable—a bird may bite with little to no warning. For this important reason, I strongly advise you to never allow a bird to perch on the shoulder of a child, no matter how closely bonded the two may seem, and never allow visitors to hold your bird in this way—even if they are comfortable with it. The effects could be disastrous, leaving you open to a lawsuit and possibly even being forced to euthanize your bird. Only you can decide if you are willing to allow your bird to sit on your own shoulder, but know the risks and use good judgment. Even if you normally allow your bird to perch in this way, return him to his cage immediately if you notice a mood change, no matter how subtle.

Parrot experts disagree on whether owners should let their birds perch on their shoulders.

A Lost Cause?

Although a microchip is a smart safety measure, it should never be the only step a bird owner takes to prevent theft or escape. It is also vital that owners keep cages securely closed whenever they cannot properly supervise their pets. Doors and windows should never be left open when birds are allowed to roam freely, and these barriers should always be locked when you are asleep or away from home. A Senegal certainly isn't the most expensive parrot, but these popular little birds can fetch decent prices for those inclined to take advantage of unsuspecting owners by way of theft. So also be discriminating about the people you allow into your home or even tell about your bird.

If your Senegal is ever lost or stolen, another excellent means of identification is probably the simplest one: a photograph. Take lots of pictures of your Senegal parrot, focusing on any distinguishing markings he may have. If he talks, also consider using a video camera to record him repeating his most commonly spoken words and phrases. These can all be powerful pieces of evidence to prove ownership if ever needed.

If you ever discover that your bird is missing, contact your local law enforcement authorities immediately. Gather your photographs of your bird, and post flyers in as many places as possible. The best spots are pet stores, veterinary hospitals, and animal shelters, but don't stop there. Look online for bulletin boards that list missing pets, or find newspapers that do the same. You can even try contacting your local television and radio stations to see if they would be willing to help spread the word. The chances of locating a lost or stolen bird may be minimal, but they are much better than if you take none of these important steps.

Screaming

Like biting, screaming can be incredibly annoying for parrot owners, as well as for those around them. Although a Senegal is a fine candidate for apartment life, a screaming habit that isn't dealt with swiftly could cost you in your relationships with your neighbors and fines from the police. You could even be forced to find a new place to live if the problem continues.

The first step in stopping screaming is to make sure that your bird is screaming for attention and not due to pain from an illness or injury. A quick trip to the vet can help rule out the latter possibilities. As soon as your bird receives a clean bill of health, you can assume that your Senegal is seeking attention with this behavior.

Remember, giving your parrot attention when he screams will only reinforce the behavior. If he starts screaming when you are in the room because he wants out of his cage, for instance, walk away. This doesn't mean that you should stay away for long periods. On the contrary, remain within earshot so that you can monitor your bird's reaction. If he continues screaming, wait. As soon as he stops, re-enter the room and praise him for being quiet. He will quickly link your return with his present behavior. If he does anything other than screech (like speak, flap his wings, lower his head), open the cage door and continue to praise him. If he screams, leave the room once more. Your consistency should pay off eventually if you are dedicated to this exercise.

When my son was a toddler and would start screaming, I encouraged him to use his words to express how he was feeling. You may also try to teach your bird to use his words in a similar way. He may not be as straightforward as an angry toddler, but you can definitely teach him that asking for attention with words is far more productive than screaming. When you re-enter the room, say *hello* or *good boy* (or whatever phrase your bird may already know) as you reappear. He just might begin to use this phrase instead of screaming when he wants your attention.

Some aviculturists recommend using a water bottle to squirt a screaming bird in the hope of discouraging screaming. I find this both harsh and counterproductive. If your Senegal enjoys misting, this will either change his mind about what should be an enjoyable pastime (his bath) or reward him for his screaming. It will also

Giving your poicephalus plenty of attention and toys is the best way to prevent a screaming problem.

do nothing to discourage him from screaming when you aren't home. Instead, catch your bird when he is behaving properly and reward him for that rather than punishing him for behaving badly.

Chewing

Chewing is not only a normal avian behavior, but in many species, including poicephalus parrots, it is also a necessary one. Although Senegals are not among the most voracious chewers, they certainly enjoy using their beaks to break open nuts and seeds, grind down wooden toys and branches, and if given the opportunity, reduce your cherished belongings to firewood. The key here is giving your parrot ample prospects for using his beak in appropriate ways and keeping items you do not wish him to chew out of his reach. It really is as simple as that.

If your poicephalus parrot appears to have an extreme penchant for destroying the toys and perches within his cage, your job is to provide him with an even more abundant supply of chewing objects and watch him like a hawk whenever he

is outside his cage. Because chewing is a natural and healthy behavior, you do not want to discourage it but instead direct it to suitable materials. Hardwoods may work best for this, but because the poicephalus beak may have some trouble cutting through these denser branches, you just might have better luck with softer woods from which your bird can derive more chewing pleasure—even if he does go through them more quickly.

Take advantage of items that cost you nothing, such as empty paper towel tubes or popsicle sticks. Remove

When a Senegal pinpoints, or contracts his pupils repeatedly, he is paying close attention to something.

Senegal Parrots

the debris from your bird's cage promptly to prevent splinters or other injuries. Also, recycle any salvageable parts of his old toys when he has chewed the rest of them to oblivion. This will help you build a toy-making kit, which will make providing new toys a fun project instead of a costly burden to your budget.

Some owners find that birds release tension through chewing. Therefore, birds kept in their cages for long periods each day are more prone to this behavior. If you are finding it difficult to keep up with your Senegal's chewing habits, consider allowing him more time outside his cage. Also, allowing him to fly within your home and get more exercise may also help reduce his overall stress level and desire to chew.

Feather Plucking

Of all the problem behaviors that commonly affect parrots, feather picking may be the most difficult on the owner. While bites hurt and screaming can be ear piercing, few things are more distressing than watching your bird pull the feathers from his body. Moreover, feather plucking, also called feather picking, can be an extremely challenging problem for owners to solve. Preventing this problem before it begins is highly preferable to reversing it. In addition to pulling out feathers, some birds continue to pick at their skin once the feathers are gone, mutilating themselves to a point

where infection and disease become dangerous side effects to this neurotic habit.

The most common reason parrots pluck feathers is boredom. A bird kept in his cage for long hours will often overpreen. Birds may also pick due to separation anxiety, hormones, or a multitude of other underlying problems. Unfortunately, identifying the root of the problem is only the beginning of finding a solution. Correcting the trigger alone is unlikely to solve your feather-picking problem once it has begun. A feather-plucking parrot is very similar to a person who starts biting her fingernails during a particularly nerve-racking time. Even after the stressor is gone, the habit still remains.

Because feather picking is also a symptom of several avian illnesses, contact your veterinarian the moment you notice your bird pulling out feathers. Once you can rule out disease, you can discuss a plan to discourage your Senegal from picking. Even if a physical cause is found, however, it is still vital to implement a strategy to treat the feather-picking behavior. Once a bird gets in the habit of plucking, he may not stop after the physical cause is eliminated.

If your Senegal is picking in response to separation anxiety, try leaving the television or radio on whenever he must be left alone. New toys can also provide a positive distraction for your bird. If boredom appears to prompt your parrot's picking, consider doing some extracurricular training. Teach him some tricks or new words and praise him lavishly for any participation. He just may start spending his cage time practicing these new activities instead of reverting to destructive behaviors like feather picking. Keeping your Senegal entertained is the easiest way to prevent behavioral picking in the first place.

You may likely find the solution to be a product of trial and error. Some birds respond well to having their cages moved to a different location in the home; with others, this may possibly worsen the problem. Bathing your bird more often can also reduce his urge to overpreen. Some parrots pick when they aren't getting enough sleep, so providing your Senegal with a cage cover could help. Watch him closely and do whatever works best for him.

If you cannot seem to solve the problem on your own, employ the help of a professional. Your veterinarian or an avian behaviorist can suggest dietary changes that might help combat the problem. These individuals should also be able to tell you what strategies should be avoided altogether. For example, some websites suggest spraying a feather-picking parrot with strong-tasting deterrents, such as mouthwash. Because alcohol is a common ingredient in most of these products, using them can actually cause your bird pain, and they are also usually ineffective in stopping the problem. In extreme situations, behavior-altering drugs can be prescribed to stop a chronic feather plucker. These should only be used as a last resort and as a temporary solution. Your ultimate goal should still be the discontinuance of the behavior through a nonchemical approach.

Need to Travel? No Fear!

Helping your Senegal overcome his fear of entering a carrier or travel cage can make vet visits a much less stressful undertaking for both you and your bird. Introduce the carrier before your bird must be put in it to avoid a rushed experience with a long-lasting impression. First and foremost, you must be patient. Expecting your parrot to hop right into a carrier is impractical. Instead, allow him to investigate the open enclosure on his own. Leave treats inside, and don't close the door the first few times he enters. This will help him form a positive association with the carrier. When he enters, praise him and continue to offer verbal and edible rewards as you begin closing the door for short periods. Eventually, he will begin to see his carrier as a home away from his cage.

Bird Body Language

One Foot Up

A bird sitting on one foot is relaxed. Birds who feel secure in their environments typically sleep with one foot raised up into their feathers and their heads turned into their back feathers or tucked under one wing. If you have adopted or rescued your Senegal—or even if you have purchased your parrot as a baby—seeing him sitting on a single foot is an excellent indication that he is feeling at home.

Beak Grinding

Every evening, predictably around nine o'clock, my parrots begin grinding their beaks. Beak grinding is an indication that a bird is feeling safe and secure, and it is usually done when he readies himself for sleep. This is often my first sign that I need to turn down the lights and think about heading to bed. The sound is amazingly specific, similar to a person grinding her teeth. This isn't surprising because a bird makes this sound by scraping his upper mandible against the lower mandible in an identical way to teeth grinding. If I happen to miss the hint, though, my Senegal-Meyer's parrot isn't afraid to be less subtle and say, "'Night, 'night," before he nods off to sleep.

Fluffing Feathers

Feather fluffing is a dual-purpose gesture. Sometimes it is purely physical,

When your Senegal lowers his head, he probably wants to be petted or scratched.

done to shake away any dander or dirt particles that have loosened during preening. At other times, though, it is a means of releasing tension. This can be very telling during the bonding process. After handling your new Senegal, watch him whenever you set him down. If he ruffles his feathers immediately, it probably means that you pushed him a little too far. If he waits about 30 seconds or so, you are likely moving along at just the right pace. A minute or more, however, indicates that you should try holding your parrot for longer periods or maybe start working with him in other ways, such as training. Beware if your Senegal consistently stays fluffed up for longer periods, though. This can be a sign that he is either chilled or sick.

Head Bobbing and Lowering

Head bobbing is an attention-seeking behavior, but the reason for wanting the attention can vary. In the wild, head bobbing is part of a parrot's courting ritual. Companion parrots sometimes bob in reaction to a health problem. Birds kept in cages that are too small or ones kept in their cages for too long can develop obsessive head-bobbing habits. A Senegal may also bob his head along with more threatening gestures as a means of appearing intimidating. Bear in mind that a parrot need not be large to pack a powerful pinch, so watch for those other signs before you reach out to scratch your bird.

A lowered head is typically a safe signal that your Senegal is ready for some petting. He may ruffle his feathers and expose a specific area of his head or neck to make reaching these spots easier for you. My MacLeod will put his head down immediately whenever my husband takes him out of his cage and rests Mac on his shoulder.

Tail Fanning

Tail fanning is usually an aggressive behavior. A Senegal fanning his tail is most likely trying to appear bigger and scarier than he actually is. Fanning may also be done to impress a bird of the opposite sex. (Think of a peacock showing off his fancy feathers.) This is another behavior that is an even greater warning when accompanied by other threatening behaviors. So listen to what your parrot is trying to tell you and back off.

Pinpointing (Contracting Pupils)

I always know when my Senegal parrot is learning something new. Usually I'm able to tell just by looking into his eyes. When Mac is paying close attention, his pupils, like most parrots', will contract repeatedly. This is known as pinpointing. This is hardly the only time birds pinpoint, though. It can be a sign of aggression, excitement, nervousness, or pleasure. The common thread appears to be the intensity of the emotion. To link the gesture to the correct mood, look for other body language cues. If your Senegal is crouching with his beak open, standing tall, or fanning his tail, step back and give him some space. If he is lowering his head and leaning in your direction, he is probably asking you to scratch him.

Regurgitating

You may be surprised to know that for parrots, regurgitation is actually a sign of affection. In the wild, this gesture is typically reserved for a bird's mate. Because pet birds often bond most closely with their owners, however, they often perform this unusual offering for their favorite human. Although it can be distasteful to witness–particularly for the unsuspecting recipient–owners should never admonish their parrots for regurgitating. This is a normal behavior. If you find that it makes you nauseous, the best thing you can do is ignore it altogether. Gasping or chastising will often just reinforce the behavior.

It is important to know the difference between normal regurgitation and vomiting due to illness. Affection regurgitation is only done in the presence of another individual, be it a fellow bird or an owner. The expelled substance is good digestible food. Vomit, on the other hand, may consist of whole pieces of food or undigested food. The vomited material may also contain blood or parasites, and it will often be an unusual color or emit a strong odor. A sick bird will vomit 10 to 20 minutes after eating, whether in the presence of another individual or not.

Eye pinpointing is a signal of some type of intense emotion; look for other body language cues to determine the correct cause.

Resources

Organizations

American Federation of Aviculture
P.O.Box 7312
N. Kansas City, MO 64116
Telephone: (816) 421-3214
Fax: (816)421-3214
E-mail: afaoffice@aol.com
www.afabirds.org

Avicultural Society of America
PO Box 5516
Riverside, CA 92517-5516
Telephone: (951) 780-4102
Fax: (951) 789-9366
E-mail: info@asabirds.org
www.asabirds.org

Aviculture Society of the United
Kingdom
Arcadia-The Mounts-East Allington-
Totnes
Devon TQ9 7QJ
United Kingdom
E-mail: admin@avisoc.co.uk
www.avisoc.co.uk/

The Gabriel Foundation
1025 Acoma Street
Denver, CO 80204
Telephone: (970) 963-2620
Fax: (970) 963-2218
E-mail: gabriel@thegabrielfoundation.org
www.thegabrielfoundation.org

International Association of Avian
Trainers and Educators
350 St. Andrews Fairway

Memphis, TN 38111
Telephone: (901) 685-9122
Fax: (901) 685-7233
E-mail: secretary@iaate.org
www.iaate.org

The Parrot Society of Australia
P.O. Box 75
Salisbury, Queensland 4107
Australia
E-mail: petbird@parrotsociety.org.au
http: //www.partosociety.org.au

Emergency Resources and Rescue Organizations

ASPCA Animal Poison Control Center
Telephone: (888) 426-4435
E-mail: napcc@aspca.org (for non-
emergency, general information only)
www.apcc.aspca.org

Bird Hotline
P.O. Box 1411
Sedona, AZ 86339-1411
E-mail: birdhotline@birdhotline.com
www.birdhotline.com/

Bird Placement Program
P.O. Box 347392
Parma, OH 44134
Telephone: (330) 722-1627
E-mail: birdrescue5@hotmail.com
www.birdrescue.com

Parrot Rehabilitation Society
P.O. Box 620213
San Diego, CA 92102
Telephone: (619) 224-6712
E-mail: prsorg@yahoo.com
www.parrotsociety.org

Petfinder
www.petfinder.com

Veterinary Resources

Association of Avian Veterinarians
P.O.Box 811720
Boca Raton, FL 33481-1720
Telephone: (561) 393-8901
Fax: (561) 393-8902
E-mail: AAVCTRLOFC@aol.com
www.aav.org

Exotic Pet Vet.Net
www.exoticpetvet.net

Internet Resources

African Parrots
proaviculture.com/africanparrots.htm

AvianWeb
www.avianweb.com/

BirdCLICK
www.geocities.com/Heartland/
Acres/9154/

Choosing Among Poicephalus Species
www.geocities.com/Heartland/
Plains/2072/poicephalus.html

HolisticBird.org
www.holisticbird.org

The Parrot Pages
www.parrotpages.com

Parrot Parrot
www.parrotparrot.com/

Poicephalus Main Page
www.wingscc.com/aps/poicep.htm

Conservation Organizations

Kakapo Recovery Programme
www.kakaporecovery.org.nz

Loro Parque Foundation
Avenida Loro Parque s/n - 38400
Puerto de la Cruz
Tenerife, Canary Islands
Spain
Telephone.: +34 922 37 38 41
Fax: +34 922 37 50 21
www.loroparque-fundacion.org

Macaw Landing Foundation
P.O. Box 17364
Portland, OR 97217
www.macawlanding.org/index.shtml

ProAves
www.proaves.org/sommaire.
php?lang=en

Rare Species Conservatory Foundation
www.rarespecies.org/

World Parrot Trust (UK)
Glarmor House
Hayle, Cornwall TR27 4HB
Telephone: 444 01736 751 026
Fax: 44 01736 751 028
E-mail: uk@worldparrottrust.org
www.worldparrottrust.org

World Parrot Trust (USA)
P.O.Box 353
Stillwater, MN 55082
Telephone: (651) 275-1877

Fax: (651)275-1891
E-mail: usa@worldparrottrus.org
www.worldparrottrust.org

Magazines

Bird Talk
3 Burroughs
Irvine, CA 92618
Telephone: 949-855-8822
Fax: (949) 855-3045
www.birdtalkmagazine.com

Good Bird
PO Box 684394
Austin, TX 78768
Telephone: 512-423-7734
Fax: (512) 236-0531
E-mail: info@goodbirdinc.com
www.goodbirdinc.com

Parrots Magazine
Imax Ltd.
Riverside Business Centre
Brighton Road, Shore-by-Sea,
BN43 6RE
Telephone: 01273 464 777
E-mail: info@imaxweb.co.uk
www.parrotmag.com

Senegal Parrots

Index

Boldfaced numbers indicate illustrations.

A
aspergillosis, 76–77
attention requirements, 19

B
bathing, 37–38, 62–63, **62**
beak care, 65
beak grinding, 101
behavior. *See* body language;
    temperament and behavior
behavior problems, 93–100. *See also*
    training
    biting, 93–95
    chewing, 98–99
    feather plucking, 99–100
    screaming, 96–98
BHA (butylated hydroxyanisole), 51
BHT (butylated hydroxytoluene), 51
birdseed diets, 45–48
biting, 93–95
black-winged Jardine parrot, 11
body language, 100–103
    beak grinding, 101
    fluffing feathers, 101–102
    head bobbing and lowering, 102
    one foot up, 100–101
    pinpointing, 102
    regurgitating, 102–103
    tail fanning, 102
brown-headed parrot, 12, **12**, 14, 16
butylated hydroxyanisole (BHA), 51
butylated hydroxytoluene (BHT), 51

C
cage covers, 40–41
cage liners, 36–37

cages, 24–28, **24**
    accessories, 26–27
    cleaning, 41
    placement, 27–28
    selection, 24–26
    territoriality and, 93, 94
Cape parrot, 12–13, **13**
carbohydrates, dietary, 56
chewing, 98–99
children
    caregiving by, 26
    and feeding, 46
    and grooming, 64
    parrots as pets for, 18
    and training, 90
    and veterinary visits, 76
chlamydiosis (psittacosis), 77–78
clubs and societies, 104
companionship, 15
conditioning perches, 35
conservation organizations, 105–106
corncob bedding, 37
crossbred *Poicephalus* parrots, 9, **9**
cuttlebone, 40

D
dairy products, 54, 55
diet, 42–59
    basic nutrients, 44–45
    birdseed as, 45–48
    feeding schedule, 56
    foods to avoid, 54
    fruits and vegetables, 52–55
    human foods, 55–57
    and life span, 20
    during molting, 69
    pelleted foods, 48–52, **49**
    preservatives in, 51–52
    supplements, 57–58
    water, 58–59

Dedication

To Mac, Jake, and Raff. No one has taught me more about parrots than the three of you. Love ya, guys!

About the Author

Tammy Gagne is a freelance writer who specializes in the health and behavior of companion animals. She is an experienced aviculturist and a regular contributor to several national pet care magazines. In addition to being an avid bird lover, she has also owned purebred dogs for more than 25 years. She resides in northern New England with her husband, son, dogs, and parrots.

Photo Credits